ADVANCE PRAISE

"Physicians have a wide gap between what we are capable of understanding and what we actually understand. When discussing an important topic like disability insurance, the space between those things creates risk. Disability Insurance for Physicians is the answer for closing that gap and reducing that risk. It should be required reading for physicians."

—DR. JEREMY PYLE, PLASTIC SURGEON

"I sustained a life-altering diagnosis during residency that put my future career in jeopardy. Billy helped me navigate obtaining affordable and comprehensive own-occupation disability insurance. He has been extremely accessible and supportive. I will continue to recommend Mr. Gwaltney— and this book—to those looking for knowledge, expertise, and integrity."

—DR. MEREDITH DUKE, SURGEON

"As this book confirms, Billy is the physician's disability insurance expert. He provides clarity about the key parts of specialty own-occupation disability insurance, giving young physicians confidence about purchasing it. He takes a topic that can be confusing and provides education and expertise to make it easy."

—**MR. DAN SULLIVAN,**
FOUNDER AND PRESIDENT OF STRATEGIC COACH

"Getting proper disability insurance is one of the most critical ways that a physician can set themselves up for financial security and peace of mind. Billy has been working with me for years since I was a resident physician. His knowledge, expertise, and experience has led to this concise and yet comprehensive book that every physician should take a few minutes to read. This is not a review. It is a call to action. Read it, and set yourself up for success!"

—**DR. MICHALE OK,** ANESTHESIOLOGIST

"I am thankful for having met Billy, who has been a staunch advocate for me and my family during my difficult time with a disability. He fought for me more than I fought for myself. Billy is the disability insurance expert. If you're a doctor looking for coverage, read this book."

—**DR. NAGUIB FARAH,** EMERGENCY PHYSICIAN

"It has been wonderful to work with Billy in the selection of my disability plan. He is very trusted and always available for questions or concerns. With this book, he's providing a great service to professionals, who are not often taught about disability insurance in school."

—**DR. RISA HURWICH,** PEDIATRIC DENTIST

"As a busy surgeon in a fast-evolving industry, I found myself overwhelmed when it came to choosing the most suitable disability insurance options for me. This book is for physicians who want to be sure their insurance is done right. Billy has been my broker for years—he knows disability insurance like I know surgery. Not only is he very responsive, but he's also a man of exemplary character who has become a trustworthy friend. Billy can only reach so many in person, and this book allows all providers the opportunity to benefit from his experience."

—**DR. GEORGE AZAR,** ORTHOPAEDIC SURGEON

"It's so easy to mess up my disability insurance, and I didn't know who to trust. As a physician, there are a plethora of people in this business, who reach out constantly and court you with fancy dinners, and I really didn't feel like any of my questions were ever answered sufficiently to make an informed decision. Then I met Billy and he made it easy and solved my problem. This book is long overdue."

—**DR. MICHOLE DEESING,**
CHILD AND ADOLESCENT PSYCHIATRIST

DISABILITY
INSURANCE *for*
PHYSICIANS

DISABILITY INSURANCE *for* PHYSICIANS

A **NO-NONSENSE** GUIDE
TO **PROTECTING** YOUR
MOST IMPORTANT ASSET

BILLY GWALTNEY

LIONCREST
PUBLISHING

DISABILITY INSURANCE FOR PHYSICIANS
A No-Nonsense Guide to Protecting Your Most Important Asset

ISBN   978-1-5445-3986-7   *Hardcover*
          978-1-5445-3987-4   *Paperback*
          978-1-5445-3988-1   *Ebook*

CONTENTS

To Ann Marie, an awesome wife and my best friend

And to Jesus, my beginning and end

INTRODUCTION

PHYSICIANS ARE SOME OF THE HARDEST WORKING PEOPLE I've ever come across. In particular, physicians in training (i.e., in residency or fellowship) are the epitome of the phrase "overworked and underpaid."

I have significant admiration for residents and fellows who endure this training to become excellent at caring for the rest of us. It's one of the main reasons I love what I do. Providing the best disability insurance to young physicians feels like a calling, and I find myself wanting to be the best ever at it.

The reason I'm writing this book is to make it easier for busy, overworked residents and fellows to take care of this important foundational issue—private disability insurance—before it gets more complicated.

More specifically, my first goal with the book is to provide education (i.e., clarity) to young physicians on the topic of disability insurance: why people buy it, how it works, and what the key definitions mean.

My second goal is to then explain how these facts can impact physicians personally. In other words, I want to show you what usually happens if someone is disabled with good coverage, what usually happens if someone is disabled without good coverage, and finally, what the process is for buying good coverage if they decide to.

It's become clear to me in my experience that often education is not enough. For example, when a physician educates a patient about the patient's condition, the physician usually—hopefully—has some sort of pathway for how to make the problem better. Or at least manageable. Maybe they even have a way to solve the problem completely.

There have been numerous times in my life when I needed so much more than just an education. I needed to know what to *do* with the information. This usually requires an expert! If you know what you need but don't know how to get it, that's no different ultimately than not knowing you need it in the first place.

Personal confession time: I used to be significantly overweight. I had managed it for most of my life since college, but in 2010, it got to the point that my wife actually begged me to see a bariatric surgeon near us in Charlotte, North Carolina. I had recently been told I had type 2 diabetes, and we were past the typical diet and exercise stuff. She told me I needed something more drastic, and deep down I knew this was true. So I agreed, figuring I had nothing to lose.

When I visited the surgeon, the medical staff informed me about gastric bypass surgery and who it was for. They also did some body measurements and ran some blood and urine tests.

In a follow-up visit, my wife and I met with the surgeon again, and he further educated us about gastric bypass surgery. But I didn't really start paying close attention until he then gave me the hard truth about my current situation: the test results were in, and they were *not* good. I was more than one hundred pounds overweight with type 2 diabetes (which I already knew) and cholesterol (triglycerides in particular) so high the blood test didn't register it. It was like my blood was gravy. My wife started tearing up right there.

The surgeon could have stopped at this point; he had "educated" me about how unhealthy I was. But thankfully, he didn't stop. He kept going because he knew something needed to change. He shared his expertise as an MD about the test results (i.e., what would likely happen without intervention). And then he offered me a solution that I needed more than I realized. He told me I was the perfect candidate for gastric bypass surgery. He gave me hope.

A cynic might say, "He told you to have surgery because he's a surgeon and surgeries are how he gets paid." Factually this is true: surgeons get paid for doing surgeries. But this did not negate the fact that I needed the surgery, that his solution was *exactly* the right call for my situation.

So I took his feedback, thought it over for a short while, and then had the surgery. And he got paid. And I lost one hundred pounds, was no longer type 2 diabetic, and my cholesterol dropped dramatically. Now, thirteen years later, I'm actually 110 pounds lower than the pre-surgery weight, have continued to work out, and I feel great. Perhaps more importantly, my wife thinks I'm smoking hot! (Okay, I added that without asking her specifically, but I'm pretty sure she thinks this.)

Why do I share this humbling story? My point is that with certain topics, while we do need education, often we need much more than education. We need interpretation of what the terms mean, even if it might be uncomfortable. And then we need a prescription—a solution—from an expert for how to take care of the issue at hand. In my case, it was a bariatric surgeon (who later became a client) who came along and provided me with the perfect solution.

Call me corny but I believe the same applies to disability insurance: education is just not enough. Based on feedback I've received from thousands of physicians across the country, disability insurance is one of the most perplexing, confusing, and even dreaded topics they encounter—it's weird, it's quirky, and it's just complicated enough to make them want to never deal with it.

Furthermore, they have no idea who to talk to about it, much less who they can trust. I totally understand this. I've been around insurance and financial services salespeople for over thirty years. Most of them I would not buy from. But some are solid. The downside is that few of the solid ones specialize in disability insurance. They avoid it for the same reason physicians avoid it: again, **it's weird, it's quirky, and it's just complicated enough to make you want to never deal with it.**

My calling is to bring clarity and confidence to this dreaded topic. For some reason, I love it. I'm not sure why. Maybe it's because so few others like it. You may call it crazy. I call it job security.

With all of this in mind, I hope you receive this book as not just an education but a recipe, a concrete solution, for your private specialty own occupation disability coverage from an expert.

HOW I BECAME A DISABILITY INSURANCE BROKER

I didn't start out as a disability insurance broker. I actually wanted to be a Wall Street guy, a money tycoon. While finishing my bachelor's in finance with a minor in economics, I joined a financial planning firm and did general financial planning, including life insurance, investments, budgeting, overall retirement planning, and education planning.

But from day one, I was confronted with a difficult conundrum, and it was something I wrestled with until about 2009. *I need to grow my business,* I would think to myself. *But how can I sit in front of someone and tell them with a straight face that I know everything, that I have the answers to all their possible questions? How can I be an expert at retirement planning, college planning, life insurance, and disability insurance? There's no way.*

Ultimately, like with many physicians nowadays, the financial services world runs on a "you eat what you kill" model. The more clients you bring in, the more money you make. It is in that context that I became a Chartered Financial Consultant, a Chartered Life Underwriter, and a Registered Employee Benefits Consultant. But even though I landed all these exciting designations, frankly I was still just an average advisor. That's because I was never entirely comfortable with my identity and how the market saw me. I was, as they say, a jack of all trades but a master of none.

In 2009, finally I started specializing in disability insurance, and it felt like walking into a tailor's store to get fitted for a suit and finding that it already fit me perfectly, as if the tailor had designed it with my measurements before I showed up. I started reading the contracts and terms and understanding the key elements of, and differences between, the top contracts. I also started talking with physicians and found there was a significant need, particularly among young trainees. They were looking for someone they could trust to help them set up their policies in the way they needed. But there just weren't many such people out there who they felt they could turn to.

It struck me that maybe I could fill that gap. Then one night, something happened that made me realize this was indeed my calling.

I live in North Carolina, and when it snows in the South, nobody goes anywhere. We stock up on toilet paper and bread and hunker down until we can see the streets again. So, on this one cold afternoon when it was due to snow, my young daughter started having extreme pain in her abdomen. It was appendicitis. At 9:00 p.m., under a threatening sky, we had no choice but to bring her to the hospital.

When we got there, the place was a ghost town, except for a couple of doctors and their team who now surrounded my daughter. They told us they needed to take her in for surgery. Not tomorrow when the roads cleared up from the snow, but tonight. Even though I was focused on my daughter and praying she would be okay, I remember also taking notice of just how well the medical personnel handled the situation and took care of her. The nursing staff was awesome. But in particular, the surgeon and hospitalist were amazing in how they interacted with my family and especially my daughter. It was like they said, "Hey, Ava, we've got you. You're going to be fine."

Physicians. As an independent broker serving this particular profession, helping them get disability insurance coverage, these would be my people. Now I was getting an up-close glimpse into their lives. I saw how hard they worked and how much they did for their patients. The last thing they needed from me, as someone trying to sell them an insurance product, was a typical broker attitude.

Again, I had been around insurance folks for a long time. I thought of all the people I had encountered in the world of insurance and financial services: a lot of ego-driven guys, some of them ex-jocks. Their whole demeanor seemed to convey distance and an uneven power dynamic: *I don't go to my clients, they come to me. I only meet with people at certain times of day. I call the shots, and they have to do what I want.*

I realized, then and there, that these physicians, who I was seeing in action, didn't owe me anything. Rather, the onus would be on me to meet them where they were and as they were, to give them the guidance and help they craved. I vowed to be there for them all the way through. If they needed to talk, I would do all I could to get on that call.

A BROKER IN A BOOK

To better understand specialty own occupation disability insurance and identify the right policy for your needs, either you can listen to a dozen podcasts (like my *Cover Your Assets* podcast) or sit down and read this book, even just the key points. I have designed it so that it's the closest thing to meeting with a good broker and having your questions about disability insurance answered.

That said, I would caution against taking this book and trying to buy a policy without ever speaking to someone. Contracts are complicated! As I tell anyone who will listen, "The devil is in the details." These contracts can have addendums and amendments and endorsements that supersede previous sections of the document. It's always wise to consult with an expert.

If you're a physician in training, I sincerely hope that you heed the call to get your own private specialty own occupation disability insurance coverage. But it's also important that you get the *right* kind and not make an inferior policy choice. Read on and find out how.

IF YOU DON'T READ ANYTHING ELSE

IF, FOR WHATEVER REASON, YOU CAN'T JUMP RIGHT INTO the following chapters, I encourage you to just take a moment now to read this one-page summary:

1. As a young physician, your most important asset isn't an investment or real estate portfolio—it's your ability to earn a good income performing your specialty. This asset is potentially worth eight figures, and insuring it makes business sense. But insurance that truly protects your income and safeguards your quality of life isn't easy to find. The "devil is in the details" as they say, and the focus of this book is to make it easy for these details to be handled well. There are two types of long-term disability policies:

    a. Private individual disability policies, which are owned and controlled by the insured individual and offer the most comprehensive definitions (these policies are excellent if structured properly—see Chapters One and Eight).

b. Group long-term disability (LTD) policies, which are owned by an employer or association and have more restrictive definitions (these policies generally should not be your primary protection as the insured has no control—see Chapters Two and Eight).

2. Statistically, expenses increase during a claim, and the chances of being disabled are much higher than many assume. Also, group LTD policies are much more difficult to collect from. Therefore, it's strongly advised that you purchase—and keep—the maximum private specialty own occupation coverage available for your situation.

3. Every good private individual specialty own occupation policy has the following three definitions (see Chapter One for details):

a. True specialty own occupation definition of disability, which means: first, that if an injury or illness keeps you from performing the material and substantial duties of the occupation (i.e., specialty or subspecialty) you were engaged in at the time of claim, you are considered to be totally disabled; and second, that there is no penalty to your policy benefit for any income you earn in a different occupation while on claim.

b. Enhanced residual/partial benefit, which pays benefits for partial disabilities. This is activated if someone can do their occupation some of the time but not full time and their income has dropped by at least a certain percentage threshold (usually 15 percent or 20 percent) below their pre-disability income. The residual benefit will pay the insured that percentage of their policy benefit.

c. Long-term recovery benefit, which is the most important benefit that most people have never heard of before. This pays if you medically recover from a disability and return to work in your occupation/specialty, but when you return to work, your income does not "recover" to the same level as before the disability. This scenario is *very* common, especially now that physician compensation is often production driven.

4. A solid policy should be non-cancelable and guaranteed renewable, meaning the insurance company cannot cancel the policy (you can at any time, they

cannot), change the definitions, or increase the rate. One top company also has a guaranteed renewable-only contract where you can save more on the cost in exchange for the insurance company having the contractual right to increase the rate by occupation classification. Other companies may offer this in the future. (See Chapters Three and Ten)

5. Trainee discounts are the largest discounts the top companies offer and are reserved for residents, fellows, and new attendings (within the first three to six months after graduation). You keep them for life on all policy amounts. (See Chapters Three and Four)

6. Beware graded and increasing premiums. (See Chapter Three)

7. Ideally, you want to find an independent broker who specializes in disability insurance for physicians. Be sure they earn their commission (which you're paying for either way). (See Chapter Ten)

CHAPTER ONE

WHY OWN OCCUPATION
DISABILITY COVERAGE
IS SO IMPORTANT

PRIVATE SPECIALTY OWN OCCUPATION DISABILITY COVER-age is important because (a) the chances of becoming disabled are higher than most might assume and (b) the vast majority of disabilities are not catastrophic. One in four of today's twenty-year-olds can expect to be out of work for at least a year because of a disabling condition before they reach normal retirement age.[1]

According to statistics compiled by the Council for Disability Awareness (CDA), a professional female age thirty-five, normal height and weight, nonsmoker, and who leads a healthy

---

1 Social Security Administration, Disability and Death Probability Tables for Insured Workers Born in 1999 https://www.ssa.gov/oact/NOTES/ran6/an2020-6.pdf, Table A.

lifestyle has a 24 percent chance of becoming disabled for three months or longer during her working career. A professional male with the same profile has a 21 percent chance of becoming disabled. In addition, for both women and men, there's a 38 percent chance that the disability would last five years or longer, with the average disability for someone like them lasting eighty-two months.[2]

What's interesting is that it's very common for a physician to think he needs private disability insurance in case he's in a major car accident and becomes paralyzed, or for a surgeon to be concerned she might cut her finger off while using a knife. These things can happen, of course. But statistically speaking, they are not why most people become disabled. In fact, over 90 percent of disability insurance claims come not from accidents but illnesses—soft tissue diseases, musculoskeletal disorders, and conditions like lower back pain, cancer, rheumatoid arthritis, and multiple sclerosis.

With the majority of disabilities, one or more of these three scenarios are likely if you have an injury or illness: (a) you become unable to do your occupation (i.e., specialty or subspecialty) and will never return to work, (b) you are able to do your occupation part-time but cannot do it full time (i.e., partially disabled), or (c) you are unable to do your occupation for a certain amount of time but later you medically recover and return to work in your occupation.

---

2 "Disability Statistics - Disabilitycanhappen.org." September 2021 https://disabilitycanhappen.org/disability-statistic/

Let's say you're a surgeon, gastroenterologist, or oncologist, and you have a herniated disc in your back. Prior to this medical issue, you would go into the hospital or clinic every day for work and perform your specialist duties whether invasive or noninvasive. Being physically present was the expectation of your employer. But now, because of the herniated disc, you can't be physically present at your place of employment.

Are you disabled?

That's the million-dollar question, right??

If you have the right kind of private specialty own occupation coverage, the answer in this example is yes, you should be classified as totally disabled for purposes of policy benefits.

But if you do not have the right kind of policy, and instead are relying on an employer group LTD (long-term disability) policy and/or an association policy, the answer is much less clear. In fact, with many policies I've seen, the answer would be a flat-out no, you're not totally disabled.

WHAT IS THE SPECIALTY OWN OCCUPATION DEFINITION OF DISABILITY?

The **true specialty own occupation definition of disability** means two things.

First, *it means that if an injury or illness keeps you from performing the material and substantial duties of the occupation (i.e., specialty or subspecialty) you were engaged in at the time of claim, you are considered to be totally disabled.*

And second, *there is no penalty to your policy benefit for any income you earn in a different occupation while on claim.*

So let's go back to the previous example and say you have a herniated disc that prevents you from being able to go to work and perform your specialty, but you can still hypothetically work in another field—one where you would utilize your specialty training but in a different format, such as from home on your laptop. Properly designed **private own occupation disability coverage** (also known as **private specialty own occupation coverage**) would consider you to be totally disabled. It also would not penalize you for earning income through these other means (like working from home).

In contrast, employer-provided policies, association policies, and really any policy outside of a handful of true specialty occupation contracts will (a) only consider you totally disabled if you can't work *at all*, (b) penalize you if you ever earn *any* income from another source while on claim, or (c) both. In many cases, they will use your extensive education and training against you.

Let's say an internet search confirms an ophthalmologist physician is qualified to perform thirty duties. But as a surgery-focused ophthalmologist, you've streamlined your day-to-day occupation to essentially five duties that you perform over and over, with the goal of becoming the best you can at those.

A properly designed specialty own occupation policy will say that if you cannot perform the material parts of those five duties you were engaged in at the time of the disability, then you are totally disabled. You can then work in a job doing some of the other twenty-five duties an ophthalmologist is qualified to do, earn an unlimited income in that job, and still collect your full own occupation policy benefit.

Conversely, an employer policy (i.e., group long-term disability) or association policy is likely to say, in effect: "Dr. Smith, we see that you cannot perform the material parts of the five duties you were doing at that time of the disability; however, our 'research' shows that you're qualified to do thirty duties. So go find a job doing some of the other twenty-five duties you're qualified to do. In the meantime, we do not consider you disabled."

This distinction is like night and day. And it's particularly relevant for physicians, whose salaries are often higher than other professions because of specialized training and expertise. Many young physicians also have a mountain of medical school debt and need to make enough money to pay it off or at least keep it current. For this reason alone, private specialty own occupation coverage is immensely valuable and preferable to the other disability policies mentioned. But let's dig in deeper.

RESIDUAL AND RECOVERY BENEFITS

When it comes to a well-designed private specialty own occupation policy, it's vital to make sure your policy also includes a **residual benefit** and a **recovery benefit.** Often with the top contracts, this is combined into one rider called the **enhanced residual benefit** or **enhanced partial benefit.**

The **residual benefit** pays benefits for partial disabilities. In essence, this is activated if someone can do their specific occupation some of the time but not full-time and their income has dropped by at least a certain percentage threshold (usually 15 percent or 20 percent) below their pre-disability income. The residual benefit will pay the insured that percentage of their policy benefit.

So in order for residual benefits to be paid, you have to meet these two requirements:

- Show that you have suffered a loss of at least a stated percentage (usually 15 percent or 20 percent) of your net earned income before taxes but after business expenses.

- Show that you are able to perform one or more, but not all, of the material and substantial duties of your occupation; or you are unable to work in your occupation full time (contracts can vary defining full time).

Your disability doesn't have to completely debilitate you in order for you to collect benefits.

A **recovery benefit** is the most important benefit that most people have never heard of before. In fact, many agents and brokers haven't heard of it either. A recovery benefit pays if you medically recover from a disability and return to work in your specialty, but when you return to work, your income does not "recover" to the same level as before the disability. This is *very* important, especially now that physician compensation is so production driven.

Let's say for example that you make $400,000 per year *before* your injury or illness and that after being on claim for five years, you then medically recover. At that point, it's possible, even likely, that you return to work at a lower salary, say $200,000 per year. If you have a recovery benefit, then this loss in salary (or rather, the percentage) would be compared to your pre-disability income, and the insurance would then pay you that percentage of your benefit.

For the record, I have never seen recovery benefits included in a company-sponsored group LTD policy, or in association policies, or really anything outside of the top-tier private specialty contracts. In our experience, it's one of the first benefits that companies tend to remove from their cookie-cutter policies.

Not having a long-term recovery benefit is a deal killer to a quality private specialty own occupation contract.

Just look at what happened with one of our clients, a family physician in his late forties, who had a stroke. Before that, he was (if not fully healthy) healthy-ish. Certainly, he was healthy enough to obtain a policy. So, the stroke and its effects came as a great surprise.

After his stroke, he was out of work for about two years but then made a strong recovery. It was so encouraging to see. He was highly motivated to go back to work, which he ultimately did. But by the time he returned to his practice, it had almost entirely evaporated. Most of his patients had, of course, found new PCPs. He was essentially starting over.

It wasn't easy. He simply couldn't see the same number of patients he used to treat, and he likely never will. Even now, he is not as quick on his feet as he used to be. However, thanks to the recovery benefit in his policy, he has been collecting these additional benefits for nearly fifteen years. Even though he has never approached the level of income he was making before his stroke, the recovery benefits have compensated for the lower salary.

As mentioned, it's common for the top specialty disability insurance companies to combine the residual and recovery benefits into one rider called the **enhanced residual benefit.**

If the policy you're considering does not use this term, *please* be sure to read in detail about both the residual (or partial) benefit and the recovery benefit.

Warning: believe it or not, it is possible to have what you think is the best contract available with one of the top companies in the market but still not have a residual benefit and/or recovery benefit. This is why it's so important to read through the contract.

WHY DISABILITY COVERAGE SHOULD BE PRIVATE AND SPECIALTY DRIVEN

Properly designed private specialty own occupation disability coverage is an individual insurance policy that you personally own. It's a private contract between you and the insurance company. Your employer is not involved in any way with the actual underwriting or the policy itself. You don't have to disclose anything to them, and they can't require anything of you.

Also, as mentioned, with private specialty coverage, you can be disabled, collect monthly benefits, and work in a different occupation (in which there's no cap to how much you're allowed to earn). Even beyond the dollars and cents, I've seen how empowering this can be for disabled physicians who are still, in a sense, grieving the loss of the abilities they once had.

Being disabled doesn't have to be completely debilitating. Thanks to private specialty coverage, you have the power to start fresh with a new occupation and maintain your independence. You can teach at a university, do consulting or certain clinical work, or write a book. Best of all, you can make unlimited income doing it.

Moreover, once the policy is issued, the coverage can remain intact and in effect no matter where you are in the world as long as the premium is paid. So, if you purchase the policy while living and working in Ohio but eventually move to Japan and become disabled, you'll still be covered. (Please note that if disabled while overseas, you may be required to return to the US after a certain point to continue receiving benefits. Consult your specific policy as needed.)

With private specialty insurance, your policy is portable—you can take it with you wherever you go.

If designed properly, as long as you pay your premiums, the insurance company is duty-bound to continue the policy. They can never cancel it, change the definitions, or reduce the coverage.

Sounds pretty good, doesn't it?

If you're still not convinced, let me show you just how much damage can occur when you rely on an employer's policy.

CHAPTER TWO

WHAT MAKES EMPLOYER GROUP LTD POLICIES INADEQUATE

OFTEN, LARGE HOSPITALS AND HEALTH SYSTEMS, AND even some private practices, offer group long-term disability (LTD) policies. Many medical associations also offer members disability policies that are technically group LTD certificates, meaning they function in much the same way as an employer group LTD policy. In this chapter, we're going to cover how these compare to the private specialty own occupation coverage discussed in Chapter One.

Group LTD policies are designed to cover all employees regardless of their health condition. So the unhealthy—and perhaps uninsurable—person gets the same coverage as the healthiest person. On the surface, this can be a good thing. But due to adverse selection (i.e., having to cover unhealthy and healthy employees with the same policy), there are usually significant shortcomings with employer LTD policies. Unfortunately, these gaps in quality are there even if the employer says it's "own occupation" or "occupation specific."

That's because there can be a huge difference between how a group contract defines "own occupation" or "occupation specific" and how a private specialty contract defines it. Often the employer's HR folks are not aware of these discrepancies and shortcomings—they're just telling you what the insurance rep that services the group policy told them. In other words, the fault lies not with your employer. It's just the nature of the insurance world when it comes to situations like this where an employer is required to cover everyone. (Sadly, these same coverage gaps are present in various association group certificate policies that are marketed to physicians directly, even though they often require medical underwriting up front.)

Putting aside the question of who's to blame for this state of affairs, what's most important is that you understand some of the key differences between employer group LTD policies and private specialty own occupation coverage:

1. As covered in Chapter One, properly designed private coverage provides a true specialty own occupation definition of disability, meaning that if you're unable to practice your occupation (defined as the duties/specialty you're engaged in at the time of the claim) you can still work in another job and collect full policy benefits. Employer group LTD policies *do not* have this same definition (again, even if they

call it "specialty-specific," what they mean is very different from what is understood in private coverage). Rather, their definition—at best—means if you cannot perform the duties of a physician (usually a list of thirty to fifty duties) then you can be disabled. Even then it often switches after two or five years to you being unable to perform any occupation. Also, it does not allow you to earn income from another source (i.e., another job, social security benefits, etc.) without reducing or eliminating policy benefits.

2. Private specialty coverage is individual coverage, meaning you own it (i.e., you are in control), whereas employer group LTD policies are owned and controlled by the employer. With the latter, the insured has no control over terms or duration/ termination of coverage. An employer can change or discontinue coverage at any time without your consent. (Most association policies function similarly in that they are actually group certificates and not individual policies, meaning the association and/or the insurance company can discontinue the policy, change the definitions, or increase the rate at any time without your consent.)

3. Private specialty coverage—again if designed properly—does not require total disability payments before paying residual/partial benefits. Employer group LTD policies, and many association

policies, often do require total disability payments to be received before paying residual benefits. This is called an "out clause," as it's quite possible to become partially disabled without ever having been totally disabled first.

4. Private specialty coverage provides a long-term recovery benefit, which continues to pay policy benefits if you recover from a disability and return to work but your income does not "recover" to its pre-disability level. We've never seen an employer group LTD policy—or association group policy—that provides a long-term recovery benefit. As discussed in Chapter One, this is a *very* important feature.

Bottom line: group LTD policies can be much more difficult to collect from at claim time. If you were to become disabled and had to rely solely on a group policy, it's likely you'd regret not having pursued private specialty own occupation coverage.

Several years ago, I was at a conference and had dinner with a senior claims executive at one of the top specialty own occupation disability insurance companies. The company he works for is excellent in the claims adjudication process. He'll tell you this is because the insurance contract is ironclad, meaning there's very little room for them to be able to wiggle out of a claim. The contract is so strong that his department assumes, anytime a new claim is filed, that the claim is legitimate unless proven otherwise.

The benefit of the doubt...is a powerful asset that is provided by private specialty occupation coverage.

This senior claims executive also told me he started out his career as a disability claims examiner at a large insurance company that sold group LTD policies to employers across the country. When he began working there, he learned he was to find a way to deny claims at least once. Only the most obvious "catastrophic" claims were not denied. The idea was that the large majority of claims were not catastrophic, and the contract terms allowed for a *lot* of "wiggle room." They also knew that most people who were denied would not appeal, either out of ignorance or fear. If the insured filed an appeal, they often even denied it again. And only if the insured appealed a second time did they seriously consider paying the claim.

When he told me this, I must have had a look of disbelief on my face, because he said, "I'm serious. I'm not exaggerating. It really happened." Which is why he said he got out of that part of the business and now works for an insurance company that provides individual own occupation coverage.

TROUBLING STORIES ABOUT GROUP LTD

In working with thousands of physicians across the country, I've heard some pretty crazy stories about stuff they've seen or heard about when it comes to disability insurance. Often these stories are a big reason they buy their private coverage.

One that stands out is from a surgeon client who has become a good friend over the years. He told me about a colleague of his who worked in the same department. This colleague fell down the stairs in his house and hit his head. Apparently, it was a significant fall. He ended up not being able to work. He couldn't stand for long, couldn't operate, couldn't do much of *anything*.

He did not have private own occupation insurance. His employer provided him with a group LTD policy that paid 60 percent up to $20,000 a month. On paper, this sure seemed like a nice policy. So he decided he didn't need any private coverage, as the group would be plenty.

After filing the claim from the fall, he ended up being denied for the group LTD benefit because he (somehow) did not meet the threshold for their definition of disability. He was unable to fight it (he was in pretty bad shape), and his wife was having to deal with all of this and simply could not. So they had to hire an attorney to handle what should have been a straightforward disability claim.

Keep in mind that this was a group LTD policy at a very large teaching hospital that had hundreds of residents and fellows walking the halls. In a previous communication I had with the head of HR for the physician group regarding another client there, he bragged to me about their "robust" group LTD cap of $20,000 per month. He probably still uses it as a selling point to attract physicians to work there. And most of them do not know how weak this coverage really is.

So my client called me and, after updating me on his colleague, asked, "How can they deny this claim?" He was upset and he had a point. The guy was so badly injured that apparently, he couldn't even get out of bed. He was a surgeon; he needed to stand to perform his job duties. Why, indeed, were they saying he wasn't disabled?

Earlier in this chapter, I mentioned talking at length with the senior claims executive—the one who used to do claims for a large group LTD carrier. I told him about this situation. In response, he shrugged his shoulders and said, "This doesn't surprise me. When I worked in group disability claims, our approach was to deny first. If the person appeals, we deal with it *then*."

All this said, there are still certain cases where the disability is severe enough that the group LTD policy pays a benefit. But even then it often does not go as planned. For example, we had a client who had a group LTD policy through her employer that covered most of her income. She also purchased a small individual own occupation policy. She became disabled and collected her disability benefits initially from both policies. But the insurance carrier for the group policy decided to perform an audit after the first year of disability payments to her. They concluded that since she was eligible for social security disability, she had to *refund* a large portion of payments that the group carrier previously sent to her. (As mentioned, group policy benefits are almost always offset by "other income," which includes social security and worker's compensation.) Consequently, she had to write a check to pay back a large portion of her benefits. Thankfully, her individual policy did not have the other income offset, so she was able to retain all her individual policy benefits. But she still had to come up with the money to repay the other policy benefits.

With group LTD policies, the claims department has more ability to poke holes in the contract terms to avoid paying out benefits. They can require you to take all sorts of arduous steps just to access any benefit at all. Then, if you ever do receive anything, after a while they can make you start over and update the entire process to justify continuing to receive benefits and/or justify what you've already been paid.

Private specialty own occupation insurance is designed to fill the gaps that group policies do not fill. Please don't make the mistake of relying on a "robust" group LTD without supplementing it with private coverage.

I learned of a similarly painful story from another client who was a resident physician in her first year of training. She told me about a colleague she knew during her internship. He was only a few years older than her, but he became disabled six months before completing his residency. His story motivated her to buy disability insurance now rather than wait. I commended her for taking care of this important matter so early in her career and asked her to tell me more about his story.

Apparently, her colleague had not yet purchased disability coverage when he became disabled. And because his disability was permanent, he was never going to get the chance to practice his specialty. He also had significant medical school debt. As a doctor-in-training, his insurance was just a small group disability policy, which was possibly going to pay him about $1,500 per month, a fraction of his trainee salary. But his hope of receiving anything at all from the group policy hinged on all the back and forth with the claims department.

Flash forward to the young physician sitting in front of me that day. She was determined not to make the same mistake of putting off purchasing something better and supplemental to any group benefits that are available in the worst-case scenario. In particular, she was interested in an untaxed $5,000-per-month payout. If she were ever to become disabled, like her friend, she knew she would need that much to cover her bills.

SPECIALIZED COVERAGE TO THE RESCUE

I have another client named Michelle who is a surgeon. She was in great health, in the prime of her life and, apart from standard check-ups, had never even needed to go to the doctor

DISABILITY INSURANCE FOR PHYSICIANS

before. She felt bulletproof, and for good reason. But even though she didn't think she needed disability coverage, she got it anyway—thankfully, one of her mentors had persuaded her it was the right thing to do.

Good thing she took the mentor's advice, because she would later be diagnosed with a significant form of breast cancer. The cancer devastated her and wrecked her health. She received treatment and went through the claims process with the insurance company. But then she got spooked when the company started asking her for additional information for verification purposes. Even though these questions are normal, she thought they meant her provider did not believe she was truly disabled. She called me and left a frantic, tearful voicemail. At this point, she had moved across the country on her own to take a new job, and her employer did not offer any group LTD. She was very worried she wouldn't receive the benefits she needed. I called her and assured her that the follow-up questions were part of the process and everything would be okay.

Ultimately, it all worked out as expected for Michelle. Her claim was indeed paid per her policy definitions. And after surgery, radiation, and chemo, she eventually recovered and within a few years went back to work, where she was in high demand in that part of the country for her specialty.

When she went back, she started paying the insurance premiums again as if she had never been disabled. (During the time that she was receiving benefits, her premiums had been waived.)

Her policy also had something called a future insurability option (which we'll look at in-depth in Chapter Three). Not only did her provider have to keep insuring her, but they also had to give her more coverage as her career expanded more over time.

Keep in mind that had she never taken out the policy, she would likely have been uninsurable for the rest of her life. This is true for most who become disabled.

It is also worth noting that Michelle had only paid premiums for a couple of years before she needed the coverage. Ultimately, she collected *way* more from the company than she will *ever* pay them in premiums.

Buying the policy was the best financial decision she ever made.

If disabled, you too will likely collect far more than you will ever pay in premiums—even if you pay into your policy for the next twenty or twenty-five years. **If you are disabled for even one year, having private specialty own occupation disability coverage means you'll *win* financially.**

Clearly, as we've seen in this chapter, there is a *huge* difference between group LTD policies and private specialty own occupation disability coverage. Making sure you have your own private coverage as a physician is vital. It's a no-brainer.

CHAPTER THREE

INCREASING COVERAGE IN THE FUTURE

IF YOU PURCHASE DISABILITY INSURANCE WHEN YOU'RE A physician in training (which, as we've discussed, is a wise thing to do), you'll typically start at $5,000 per month of coverage. Some top companies have increased their trainee maximum to $6,000 per month. But for this example let's stick with $5,000 per month. This equals $60,000 annually post-tax (private policy benefits received are generally nontaxable as long as the premium is not deducted)—a significant sum for many if not most trainees.

However, this amount of coverage usually won't be enough as you advance in your career from resident or fellow to attending physician. For most of our clients, after they become an attending, their income grows as their production increases and/or they become a partner in a practice. They find their lane. As this happens, $60,000 (even non-taxed) likely won't cut it anymore. It doesn't give you and your family enough security. While physicians tend to have relatively high earning potential, this doesn't necessarily translate to financial security, especially if a sickness or injury leads to a disability. As we'll see throughout the book, to have one's income stopped or drastically cut can lead to financial catastrophe.

In a properly designed private specialty own occupation disability contract, you can purchase additional coverage by activating a rider that allows you to increase coverage (a) without any additional medical screening required, (b) with the same definitions included in the additional coverage, and (c) with the same trainee discount attached to the additional coverage's premium (assuming a trainee discount is on the base policy—see Chapter Four). There are two riders that the top companies use to accomplish this: the future insurability option and the benefit increase rider. They accomplish the same goal but function quite differently. Most of the top companies currently offer both riders, with you deciding up front (i.e., at the time you purchase a policy) which you prefer.

The **future insurability option** (or **FIO** for short, also known as the **future increase option rider)** enables you to increase coverage on each policy anniversary date, although there are exceptions (like graduation) when you can do an off-anniversary increase. There is an extra fee you pay on the original policy for this FIO rider and the flexibility it offers. Again, if structured properly, you'll be eligible for these increases without any additional medical screening, and with the same trainee discount and the same definitions all included. Also worth noting: the rate for the coverage increases will usually be based on the same occupation classification and state you lived in at the time you bought the original policy.

The **benefit increase rider** (or **BIR** for short, also known as the **benefit update rider** or **benefit purchase rider**) allows you to increase coverage every three years (i.e., every three years you provide your updated income and group LTD, and the underwriter confirms any additional coverage you have available to you at that point). There is usually no fee for the BIR. Similar to the FIO rider, the coverage increases do not require updated medical screening and should include the same definitions and the same trainee discount as the original base policy. However, the BIR typically includes a requirement that you accept at least 50 percent of any eligible coverage increase or they will remove the rider from the policy. Removal of the rider means any increase in coverage going forward would require a new/updated medical screening. Also, the BIR rate will often be calculated based on the state you live in at the time of the increase (not the original policy purchase state), which would be a significant negative if you live in California or Florida when you activate the BIR.

Having the FIO rider or BIR serves as an important hedge against being underinsured as your income grows over your career. For this reason, it's important for young physicians in particular to include one of these on their policy if at all possible.

HOW ARE THE FIO AND BIR CALCULATED?

As a trainee, the top disability insurance companies allow you to purchase up to $5,000 per month of initial coverage (one company recently increased their trainee maximum to $6,000 per month). But once you become an attending, they utilize a formula to calculate how much coverage you can purchase based on your total earned income. Insurance companies don't want people overinsured if they can help it. They've learned the hard way over time not to give people too much of an incentive to become "creative" about how to claim a disability.

Each company starts with a total amount of long-term disability coverage from all sources based on your earned income. Then they subtract a portion of any employer-provided group LTD, and whatever is left over is the gap you can fill with private specialty coverage.

Since private specialty disability coverage is nontaxable income, the math can look a little odd at first glance, as you're ultimately trying to replace a pre-tax salary with a non-taxed benefit. As a rough estimate for discussion purposes: for our clients who want to maximize their coverage, we can typically get them to 70 to 85 percent of their net (i.e., post-tax) pay, factoring in all coverage.

Please keep in mind that while the group LTD is much less valuable from a definition standpoint (see Chapter Two), unfortunately, it still counts against how much private coverage you can purchase. As your income increases and/or you move to an employer with no group LTD, you would be able to revisit purchasing more private specialty coverage.

For the top insurance companies, the maximum private specialty coverage they'll issue for any one physician is anywhere from $15,000/month to $30,000/month. This variation depends on the company, the state you live in, and your specialty. Also, these caps have increased over time, so ten years from now, the caps will likely be higher.

That said, insurance companies *won't* allow you to have $20,000/month of coverage just because you're willing to pay for it. The amount you can purchase is directly tied to your earned income. As mentioned earlier, insurers don't want to give people too much incentive to become disabled, which is also why they won't pay claims for self-inflicted injuries.

Once your private specialty coverage amount is issued, as long as you pay the premium, this remains the amount payable if you become disabled. At the time of claim, the top disability insurance companies will pay whatever the policy benefit is. This can work for you or against you.

For example, if Rachel becomes disabled and at the time of the claim her income is $500,000 per year but her private specialty policy benefit is still $5,000 per month, the insurance company will pay her $5,000 per month. Conversely, let's say Rachel was earning $500,000 per year and increased her private specialty coverage to $18,000 per month. Then a few years later, she went part-time and her income decreased to $250,000 per year, while she kept paying the premium for the $18,000 per month policy. If she were to become disabled at this point, the insurance company would have to pay her $18,000 per month (even though she does not qualify financially for $18,000 per month based on her reduced income at the time of claim).

It's important to remember to be proactive about increasing your coverage. Insurance companies have no way of knowing that Rachel went from making $60,000 a year as a trainee to making $500,000 as an attending. It's up to her or her broker to inform them of her new salary so they can run the calculation to confirm how much additional coverage she's eligible to purchase. As mentioned a few pages ago, if structured properly, this is like "flipping a switch" to activate the FIO/BIR on the policy.

Typically, the FIO rider can be on the policy to age forty to forty-five. The BIR often remains to age fifty-five. Each company is different, and guidelines can and do change. This is another reason it's highly advisable to work with a specialist who keeps track of these nuances.

GET INSURED LIKE IT'S 1999

As a policyholder, if you have the FIO/BIR on your policy and develop a severe medical condition—one that makes it complicated or even impossible to qualify for a new policy—you can still acquire additional coverage without having to undergo further medical testing.

This is a key reason that the FIO/BIR is so important. At whatever point you exercise it, your health status at that time will *not* be a factor. But that's only true *if* the policy has been written correctly.

The bottom line: assuming the rider has indeed been appropriately crafted, there's no need to update the medical screening. Which means you don't have to be as healthy as you were a decade earlier (a high bar that not many of us would meet!)

"OPTION" MEANS MAKING A CHOICE

I had one client, Sam, who had the BIR on his policy that allowed him to increase coverage every three years by at least 50 percent of what he was eligible for. His income kept increasing, and he simply did not want to add more coverage. He said it was annoying and a waste of money. I caught him at a bad time—he had a lot on his plate. So, against my advice, he passed on the option, and the insurance company removed the rider from his policy.

Fast-forward two years, and he was in a different job where he needed more private insurance. His income had increased significantly, and now he was at a juncture in life where he was concerned about his family's enduring financial security. His financial responsibilities were significant. He reached out to me about increasing coverage.

I told him we could do it but would have to update the medical screening—because the BIR wasn't on his policy any longer.

He went through the process, and I thought he'd be fine. He seemed healthy to me, but the underwriter discovered he had been getting neurological treatment because of chronic headaches. He went through a battery of tests.

Turns out, he was uninsurable. He could *not* get more coverage. There is still a chance that the issue can be revisited in the future, but for now, he's stuck with what he has.

Stuff happens. Life happens. And Sam just happened to have one of those policies where you have to accept additional coverage within a specific timeframe. He declined, and the decision came back to bite him—big time.

Another client, Jerry, had a different experience. He was a surgeon and had developed a slight tremor. It wasn't incapacitating, and he was still killing it at work, but he was nervous about the new tremor and had forgotten that he could increase his coverage via his policy's FIO. He reached out to me on the policy anniversary and brought up the subject with the comment, "I guess I am uninsurable."

I reviewed the policy increase and confirmed 100 percent that he had the future insurability option. He told me to max it out. Stat! I said we could definitely do that. His tremor was not bad enough (yet) to affect his work, but it was enough to notice and scare him. Thankfully, he was able to bump up his coverage, and the insurance company didn't (and couldn't) ask anything about his health (because the ability to increase coverage had been included in his coverage).

Another client, Elena, was an emergency physician who had become disabled. She had barely gotten $5,000 per month of coverage while in training—and even though she was polite, I don't think she was my biggest fan as the "insurance guy." She had basically just done it to check a box. All along, she had been reluctant and complained about it essentially every time we talked. But to her credit she got the coverage anyway...and then one day she actually needed it! As it so often does, *life happened,* and Elena became disabled soon after becoming an attending. She had to have significant surgery and was out of work for about eighteen months.

Because she had been healthy, Elena made an excellent recovery, and when she was ready to go back to work, her income was still higher now that she was an attending physician. This all happened just at the right time when her specialty in that particular part of the country was in higher demand. She actually found herself making more money than she had ever imagined.

During the claim, the one complaint from Elena was that she wished she had bought the maximum she was eligible for based on her attending income. Statistically speaking, expenses typically go up during a claim, and her situation was no different. When she came back, she asked, "Can I increase my coverage based on my higher income now?"

Statistically speaking, expenses typically go up during a claim.

I said, "Absolutely, you've got the future insurability option on your policy. That's still active now that you're back to work because you've started paying the premium again." Her premium was waived while she was receiving payout.

Medically, Elena—like Michelle in Chapter Two—is uninsurable, possibly for the rest of her life. But because she had the future insurability option on her policy, she could still increase her coverage without having to go back through any medical screenings. From a policy standpoint, her insurers saw her as just as healthy as she was when she had originally bought the policy. They bumped her up from $5,000 to close to $15,000 per month in coverage. If her illness comes back, she'll be covered and her benefit will be $15,000 per month, not $5,000 per month.

I often run into these scenarios where people want to increase coverage, and they ask if they have to be screened first. I love being able to tell them that because they had the wise foresight to include the future insurability option or benefit increase rider, they don't have to be screened. Such news is always met with a sigh of relief.

HOW MUCH DOES THE FIO AND BIR COST?

As mentioned earlier in this chapter, the top specialty disability insurance companies charge a fee for the FIO rider. While the percentage cost can feel high (often 15 percent or more of the policy's initial premium), it's relatively inexpensive from a big picture point of view. In other words, it's usually worth $20/month to be certain that you can increase your coverage every policy anniversary in the future with all parts of the contract static and no additional medical screening. It's like flipping a switch. Once your income is higher and you calculate the additional available coverage, you e-sign a form and you're done. And as your coverage increases and the FIO amount decreases, the corresponding cost of the FIO rider also decreases. So by the time you're a few years out of training, the FIO rider fee is either removed or significantly reduced.

All this said, I'm very aware of my clients' tight budget constraints as a trainee. (It's one reason I love working with physicians—living on peanut butter sandwiches and mac-n-cheese for three to seven years in order to become really good at your specialty is not easy to do. I admire that.) So I recognize that it's your money and not mine.

For those who struggle with the idea of paying an FIO rider fee, most of the top companies offer the benefit increase rider as well. This usually does not add any cost to the policy. But it does require that you increase every three years by at least 50 percent of the amount you financially qualify for. Some clients are glad to stick to a reasonable schedule of increases in exchange for no ongoing cost for the rider.

For example, if an attending has $10,000/month of coverage and at their BIR three-year anniversary they're eligible for $20,000/month, they are required to increase to at least $15,000/month or the BIR will be removed from the policy.

Also there's a slight hitch to be aware of—policyholders with a BIR are also **limited** to increasing their coverage every three years. There are certain "triggering" exceptions like graduation, losing group LTD coverage, and so on, but you can usually only activate an exception once during the three-year cycle.

So again there's a tradeoff—no fee for the BIR, but the insurance company adds some "guardrails" that dictate when and how much you must increase in order to keep the rider. A lot of our clients are fine with this schedule in order to save the fee. A lot are not.

Whether your policy has an FIO rider or a BIR, if it's structured properly, any trainee discounts applied when you originally purchased the policy will continue when you apply for increased amounts of coverage. The importance of getting the trainee discount is that once you are considered a trainee, you will always receive that discount even after you become an attending physician.

GET WHAT YOU CAN

The future insurability option and benefit increase rider are crucial features, but it shouldn't be a deal-breaker if you can't get them because of medical underwriting (which we'll cover in more detail in Chapter Eight). **Disability insurance isn't all or nothing. Always get what you can.**

There are times when someone's medical history is such that they are able to secure private specialty coverage, but the insurance company cannot allow the FIO/BIR. In other words, for the insured to add coverage in the future, the insurance company will need to verify that the insured's health situation is stable.

If an underwriter at any of the top disability insurance companies agrees to offer you true specialty own occupation coverage (of any amount, even without the FIO/BIR), it's highly advisable to consider taking it. It's a good move because it's still the best coverage, and once issued, it can never be pulled away from you. Once you pay the initial premium, the insurance company is on the hook. It's a unilateral contract, meaning *you* can walk away from it at any time, but *they* have to perform.

If your situation is stable or improves later when you're ready to increase your coverage, you can revisit the medical screening and quite possibly obtain the additional coverage. You may even be able to have the FIO or BIR added to that extra coverage.

I tell my clients, "Even though this is not the ideal outcome, it's highly advisable to get the coverage that they're offering. Put it to bed, and then we can revisit it. If later we discover there's something better, quicker, easier, more streamlined, with better definitions, then we can pivot, but in the meantime, you're not financially exposed and stuck with nothing."

CHAPTER FOUR

DISCOUNTS, AGE, AND OTHER FACTORS THAT DETERMINE POLICY COST

RATES FOR PRIVATE INDIVIDUAL DISABILITY COVERAGE are set by insurance companies and filed with each state's department of insurance. What this means is that individual disability insurance is not like real estate, where the cost can fluctuate at any given time based on market forces. The rate is the rate.

That said, there are several factors that determine the cost of your private specialty own occupation coverage. While all of our clients who are purchasing coverage choose from the same handful of top contracts, the premiums they pay for the coverage can vary widely depending on these factors. Insurance actuaries come up with these factors, so it can be a waste of energy to try to guess what they are or why they're significant.

YOUR SPECIALTY

The first, and perhaps most obvious, factor that determines the cost of coverage is your specialty. Essentially every specialty is assigned an occupation classification based on how that particular insurance company views the riskiness of that specialty. The riskier the classification, the more the specialty in that classification will pay for their coverage.

Worth noting is that certain subspecialties will have their own specific occupation classification assignment, while other subspecialties will be lumped into a particular specialty occupation classification. Again, it's useless to try to assign logic to this. It's advisable to just accept it as it is and use the information to determine which option is best for your situation. (Also I realize this might be confusing. Email me at billy@ownoccdisability.com if you have specific questions.)

For the most part, the top companies assign surgical specialties (general surgeons, vascular surgeons, orthopedic surgeons, etc.) to their riskier occupation classifications. Likewise, they assign nonsurgical specialties to their less risky occupation classifications. Each company has their own way of labeling these occupation classes. For example, one company uses the coding of 4M to 6M. Another company uses 3P to 5P. They also typically have certain preferred occupation modifiers that add certain discounts, even for riskier occupations.

One thing every company has in common is that they use their own actuaries, but these individuals see risk similarly in certain ways and very differently in other ways. The result is that the price associated with certain specialties can vary wildly within the top companies. For example, one company places dermatologists in their riskiest occupation classification (i.e., most expensive, with surgeons, anesthesiologists, etc.). Meanwhile, another top-tier company places dermatologists in their least risky classification (i.e., least expensive, with pediatricians and family physicians). From what I can tell, there's no rhyme or reason to this; it's just a difference in how they assign certain risks.

Please remember that the true specialty own occupation definition of disability means that this coverage is going to activate if you cannot perform the material duties of the specific occupation you were engaged in at the time of claim. Nothing about the cost an occupation classification pays changes how this definition will function. The only point about the occupation classification your specialty is assigned is that it impacts how much the premium will be for the coverage.

So, first and foremost, the specialty determines the occupation classification, which then plays a large role in what the cost of coverage will be.

YOUR AGE AND TOBACCO USE

Second, your age and whether or not you use tobacco will impact the rate. The younger you are when you buy, the lower the cost. If structured properly, the cost for $5,000 per month of coverage you purchase at age thirty will remain at that same level until age sixty-five or sixty-seven. If you purchase $5,000 per month at age thirty-three, then it will remain at that cost until age sixty-five or sixty-seven. Generally there is a 4 to 5 percent higher cost for each year older you are when you buy.

Also, if you do use any tobacco (smoking, smokeless, etc.), the cost will typically be 25 percent higher. If/when you can prove you've gone twelve months without any tobacco use, most of the top companies will drop you back down to the lower non-tobacco rate.

STATE OF RESIDENCE

With properly designed private specialty own occupation coverage, you're covered wherever you live and move. That's how you want it to be, of course. However, the state you live in when you buy coverage governs the rate you pay for the life of the policy. These differences in rates between states likely won't impact your ability to reach your retirement goals or send your children to the school you want them to attend. But it's something you should at least know about. Certain states (like California and Florida) can cost a good bit more than others (like North Carolina and Illinois). Again, insurance actuaries come up with this stuff in their basements, so don't waste your time trying to figure out the why or how. It's just the way it is.

Worth noting here also is that for the benefit increase rider discussed in Chapter Three, the cost for the additional coverage accessed via the BIR is often based on the state you live in when you exercise the increase. Typically, this is not a huge issue. But again, if you're planning to move to California or Florida after graduation, you might want to see if you can activate the BIR increase before you technically move to California or Florida. If you have a solid broker, they can help make this happen.

GENDER

Statistically speaking, females have a higher likelihood of becoming disabled. They also can stay disabled longer. As a result, disability insurance rates for females are higher than for males. But it's not all bad news. Females are also likely to live longer than males—my wife will probably outlive me by a long shot—and for this reason, males have higher life insurance rates. I say this not to dismiss the higher disability insurance costs for females but to help keep it all in perspective.

In the past, the top companies have offered "gender neutral" rates where both males and females pay the same rate. This is good for females and less good for males (i.e., males pay more to offset the lower cost the females are paying). These programs come and go. For the most part, as of the time of this writing, these gender-neutral rates are generally either on the way out or not available with the top companies. An expert broker will know the lay of the land regarding these opportunities when you decide to buy.

DISCOUNTS

The rate you pay can be dramatically impacted by discounts. The companies that offer the top specialty own occupation disability policies offer significant trainee discounts for residents and fellows. These range from 10 percent on the low end to 30 percent or even higher, depending on your specialty. If you purchase with a discount, it remains on the policy for life. Also, if structured properly, the discount will be applicable for all coverage increases as well.

The top companies also often offer attending discounts (for attendings who are buying a new policy). It might be through an association or an employer affiliation. These discounts are usually not quite as large as the trainee discounts; however, they're still worth having—and they remain on the policy for life.

In the current marketplace, your private specialty policy should have some type of discount on it.

CONTRACT STRUCTURE

Lastly, it's important that your policy has a level, fixed premium structure. In the insurance world, this is called "non-cancelable" (also known as "non-cancelable *and* guaranteed renewable"), which means that your policy can never be canceled by the insurance company (you can cancel at anytime, they cannot), the contract terms can never change, and the rate can never be increased until age sixty-five or sixty-seven.

Currently, one top specialty disability company offers another fixed premium policy called "guaranteed renewable" (also known as "guaranteed renewable-only"). This means that your policy can never be canceled by the insurance company, the contract terms can never change, but your rate *can* be increased by state and occupation classification. The benefit of this option is that the premium is about 15 percent less than the non-cancelable premium.

Not all of the top disability insurance companies offer the guaranteed renewable-only option. Others may in the future. Just be sure you know which one you have.

BEWARE GRADED AND INCREASING PREMIUMS

Some of the top companies offer what's called a "graded premium" option, where the premium starts off much lower than the level premium but then increases each year you have the policy. At some point in the future, after you become an attending and have the ability to pay a higher rate, you "convert" to a levelized premium. The supposed benefit of the graded premium is it allows you to afford an expensive policy while in training. The catch is that the "converted" level premium is always higher—often much higher—than what the level premium would have been from the start, meaning you trade a lower premium for a few years in exchange for *way overpaying* for thirty years.

Our clients do not choose the graded premium option, I think, because I would not choose it personally. Maybe some consider this biased advice. But my clients want my expertise. And of the top specialty disability contracts, I've not seen one that is worth significantly overpaying for compared to the others. If a top contract happens to be significantly more expensive for your situation (due to specialty, age, etc.), then it's advisable to consider one of the other top contracts that may be more affordable (instead of choosing a graded premium for the more expensive one).

One insurance company, which actually has a sub-par contract, has a premium that increases over time. Also, association policies—which are often group certificates and not individual policies—can have premiums that increase in five year increments (i.e., at age thirty, thirty-five, forty, and so on) and with discounts that are not guaranteed.

Bottom line: be sure you understand what makes up the cost of your policy. It's important to verify this in writing inside the contract, not just by what the agent/broker says. You obviously want the largest discounts, but be sure you're not unknowingly cutting corners.

WHY BUY EARLY?

For whatever reason, the insurance companies that offer the top specialty own occupation disability policies roll out the red carpet to physician trainees (residents and fellows). They do *not* roll out the red carpet, or any carpet, to attendings. It's a bit odd, actually. But there really is a legitimate incentive given to trainees to purchase coverage before graduating.

First, trainees get by far the largest discounts these companies offer for any occupation segment. The discounts are reserved for residents, fellows, and new attendings (within the first three to six months after graduation). As mentioned, once secured on your policy, you keep the discount for life on **all** policy amounts.

Second, the medical screening is usually easier because you're not required to do the in-person insurance physical. It is waived for trainees with the top companies. (Obviously, this could change in the future; an expert broker will be able to guide you to the best option.) You're still being medically screened for the best coverage. The underwriters are just doing it electronically and over the phone.

Of course, you can also wait to buy coverage once you become an attending. As long as you're still insurable from a medical underwriting approval standpoint, there's no difference between the contract definitions if you buy as an attending or as a trainee. They're the same policies. But if you purchase as an attending, (a) you'll very likely pay more for the same coverage compared to it being purchased as a trainee, and (b) the medical screening will usually be more of a hassle because the insurance physical will likely be required.

CHAPTER FIVE

ELIMINATION PERIOD, BENEFIT PERIOD, AND COLA

THE KIND OF DISABILITY COVERAGE WE'VE BEEN TALKING about is designed for *long-term* disabilities. This means that it lasts beyond an initial **elimination period**—typically, ninety or 180 days. It is, however, possible to pick an elimination period of up to a full year. A few companies have a sixty-day elimination period, but most are moving away from that because the cost is so much higher. (Some used to have a thirty-day elimination period, but that was higher still.)

The elimination period is the length of time you self-insure from the date of the diagnosis or event until the day the first payout check shows up. For example, if someone is disabled on January 1 and has a ninety-day elimination period, the first check will arrive in late April. If they have a 180-day elimination period, then the first check will come in late July.

The longer someone is willing to self-insure—cover their expenses out of pocket or from their savings—the lower the corresponding premium will be. Most of our younger clients gravitate to the ninety-day period because they haven't yet built much savings.

In contrast, many of our older clients, who tend to have built up more of a cushion, will take a good long look at the 180-day period. When you have a disability and aren't able to work, you have to consider how much money you have at your disposal to pay the bills before your benefits kick in. If a disability lasts five months and you have a 180-day elimination period, you would receive no benefits. Or if a disability lasts eighteen months and you have a ninety-day elimination period, you're going to collect fifteen months of benefits.

THE BENEFITS OF CHOOSING THE NINETY-DAY ELIMINATION PERIOD

Of course, some clients look for ways to receive a shorter elimination period without understanding that the cost would be astronomical for them. In fact, the difference between the premiums for policies with a thirty-day (when they used to be available) versus a ninety-day elimination period could be *50 to 100 percent* higher. The bottom line is that the price for a much shorter elimination period would be prohibitive—something you just wouldn't be willing to pay.

The most cost-effective option is to self-insure for the elimination period. This is, by the way, the reason so many financial advisors will tell you it's a good rule of thumb to have three to six months' salary in the bank as a cushion.

Some employers do offer short-term disability, but from what I've seen with my clients, the cost for this can be steep. Of course, some clients want to pay for short-term disability to cover things like maternity leave, which aren't technically illnesses or injuries. Either way, there's no getting around the reality that the cost for short-term coverage can be hefty—as much as a thousand dollars per month. Granted, you're not going to have to pay much out of pocket if you *do* need to use your short-term disability coverage. If you *don't* use it, however, you could be hemorrhaging money. You'd arguably be better off if you simply took that premium each month and put it in savings.

When it comes to cost-effectiveness and optimum disability coverage, the ninety-day option is the most common elimination period.

Something to keep in mind is that if you pick a shorter elimination period, the insurance company will often allow you to switch to a longer one in the future. But you can't do the opposite—go from a longer one to a shorter one. To do so, you'd have to start all over with a new policy.

In effect, this elimination period functions as a deductible on a policy, one quantified by the length of time and not dollars.

Back to our January 1st example from earlier in this chapter: the "benefits clock" after a ninety-day elimination period would start on April 1st, so you'd begin receiving your benefits toward the end of April. There is a delay because benefits are typically paid in arrears. It's like a salary: you work for a couple of weeks or a month, and then you get your paycheck.

Again, keep in mind that females generally pay more for their private specialty policy than males. That is mainly because, statistically, females become disabled more frequently and tend to stay disabled longer. As a result, females can sometimes pay premiums that are 20 to 50 percent higher than their male counterparts, depending on specialty.

According to the *Council for Disability Awareness*, a typical female (aged thirty-five, average height and weight, nonsmoker, has a professional occupation, works in an office, and leads a relatively healthy lifestyle) has a 24 percent chance of becoming disabled for three months or longer during her working career. But a male with all the same specs has a 21 percent chance of becoming disabled.

This may not seem to be that big of a difference. But in actuarial work, it is significant.

Interestingly, when it comes to gender disparity, disability insurance is vastly different from life insurance. Because females tend to live longer than

> *males, life insurance rates are significantly lower*
> *for females than males. So it tends to "come out in*
> *the wash."*

A male might pay $100 per month in premiums, and a female might pay $150 per month. There are several ways to reduce this differential. One way would be to extend her elimination period to 180 days.

THE BENEFIT PERIOD

The **benefit period** is the maximum period of time you can receive benefits for total disability, residual (i.e., partial) disability, and also recovery benefits. The most common benefit period is to age sixty-five, which was designed as the cut-off as social security and other retirement benefits would then kick in. Other benefit periods are to age 67 and age 70. Some insurance companies back in the 1980s and 1990s used to actually offer lifetime benefits. But they got clobbered in claims so the lifetime benefits went the way of the horse and buggy.

For clients who have certain pre-existing conditions, the top specialty own occupation disability companies have gotten better at offering these clients their best coverage with a shorter benefit period (i.e., a five-year or ten-year benefit period per disability). This is a significant improvement over the last decade, when these clients before then might have been a total decline, but now they can secure the best defini-tions with a benefit period that obviously isn't ideal but still covers the vast majority of private disability insurance claims.

COLA—PAY ADJUSTMENTS, NOT THE DRINK

Another critical issue when it comes to disability insurance is the **COLA—or Cost of Living Adjustment—rider.** The COLA is a supplemental rider that increases the benefit *once someone becomes disabled* in order to keep pace with inflation. This rider is paid for from the start of the policy.

Each company has its own way of calculating the COLA. Usually they have more than one COLA calculation to pick from as well. Some COLA rates are fixed (i.e., 3 percent fixed with either simple or compound interest). Others will use a floating rate of 0 to 3 percent or 0 to 6 percent based on the Consumer Price Index (CPI), the United States' national gauge of inflation.

When it comes to the COLA rider, you pick which one you want upfront. Of course, a 0 to 6 percent compounded COLA option will cost more than a 3 percent fixed simple interest COLA option.

The more robust the COLA calculator, the higher the cost.

Inflation was not much of a factor for the past decade or so—that is, of course, before COVID-19. The economic challenges that accompanied the pandemic will continue as the nation slowly emerges from it. One of the most significant long-term financial implications is (and will likely continue to be) inflation. Massive government bailouts dramatically increased spending, and other factors have led to higher prices and costs. With the COLA written into your policy, you can make sure that, if you are disabled, your benefit will have a better chance at keeping pace with the modern cost of living.

It's common for people to assume that, if they are disabled, their expenses will decrease. They're not driving as much, so they are spending less money on gas; they are at home more, so they're not paying like they used to for entertainment or eating out. Unfortunately, the logic here is misguided. Statistically speaking, expenses go up during a claim, as we saw with Elena in Chapter Three. There are always new expenses to offset any other perceived savings—healthcare and medication costs, for example.

The COLA rider comes into play particularly for younger physicians. As covered earlier in this chapter, you can elect to receive disability benefits up to a certain age—sixty-five or seventy. As of this writing, most pick sixty-five. The coverage is designed to pay benefits from the end of your elimination period for the duration of the disability up to the age selected. If someone is permanently disabled in their thirties with a benefit period to age sixty-five, they will very likely be glad they have the COLA rider on their policy.

As a rule of thumb, when I discuss this with younger clients, I tell them that if the COLA option is affordable from a budgeting standpoint, it's advisable to consider including it. If you ever have a disability that lasts, say, eighteen months, getting COLA might seem like a waste of money. But if your disability extends over several years, it could be significant.

Again, like with the elimination period, you can usually remove benefits, but you can't add them. If you start without the COLA, in most cases, you cannot add it without starting over. But if you start with it and want to reduce or remove it, that's usually relatively easy to do.

CHAPTER SIX

PSYCHIATRIC BENEFITS

THE PSYCHIATRIC BENEFIT IN YOUR PRIVATE SPECIALTY
own occupation insurance covers disabilities that are related
to addiction, depression, and anxiety. Currently, most of the
top disability companies offer a two-year benefit for psychiatric disabilities. One company has had a five-year benefit for
certain specialties. A couple of them offer it for the full benefit
period (e.g., to age sixty-five) for an extra fee.

I've heard the psychiatric benefit cynically referred to by some
as the "physician's out clause." The thought goes that a tired,
worn-down physician could say "I cannot do this any longer. I
just can't handle it. I have to tap out." If they have the psychiatric benefit in their policy, a situation like this could qualify
for benefits because the burnout would be considered a type
of depression.

This brings up the question: **what exactly does it mean for
someone to be depressed or anxious to the point that**

they can't go to work at all? And how is a claim adjudicated if someone is apparently unable to do their specialty due to depression and then says they can still teach or consult? This is where things can get muddy.

But again, a couple of top-tier disability insurance companies offer a psychiatric benefit for the full benefit period (i.e., to age sixty-five). These companies actually see this as a significant selling point for choosing them as your disability carrier, as their focus is providing this benefit for the "unforeseen life event." For example, say a pediatric surgeon has a child who dies. As a result, he can no longer bring himself to operate on children. He tries, but he just can't do it. He needs time, and he may never be able to come back. This would be a selling point for a long-term psychiatric disability benefit. If he has private specialty coverage with one of the top companies that provide this, he could collect his full benefit and still do another job like teaching at a medical school.

Sounds pretty good, right? It is, but keep in mind that the freedom and flexibility associated with this benefit doesn't necessarily come cheap. The policies that have a long-term psychiatric benefit are usually the most expensive.

In my experience, clients who can obtain coverage via medical screening are usually not as driven by this benefit. They've lived to the age of thirty or thirty-five without needing psychiatric care—or maybe only needed it for a short period after a bad breakup or while struggling with the stress of medical school exams—so they're more confident it won't come up in the future. Conversely (and unfortunately), those who may find this benefit to be important have often already been treated, either currently or in the recent past. Therefore, they are usually unable to obtain it in their policy (i.e., it will be excluded as a pre-existing condition during the medical screening, as described below).

HOW LONG DO PSYCHIATRIC BENEFITS LAST?

Again, with the top contracts typically there's a limit to the psychiatric benefit. It's either payable for the full benefit period (i.e., to age sixty-five) or limited to shorter-term benefit periods, ranging from two to five years. One company currently offers two years per occurrence. For group LTD policies through an employer, the average benefit period for psychiatric disabilities is two years.

As an FYI, if you're talking to an "insurance insider" like an actual underwriter, they may refer to the psychiatric benefit as a **"mental/nervous benefit."** I'm not sure why they refer to it this way. I wish it wasn't the case, as it can make you think there's a limit to neurological/nervous system illnesses, which is not accurate. Let me say it again just to make sure it's clear— **the psychiatric benefit does not pertain to neurological illnesses** like Parkinson's or Alzheimer's disease. These are covered under the regular disability definition.

For what it's worth, neither I nor my closest colleagues—all combined, we work with tens of thousands of physicians across the country—have seen a claim go beyond two years for anxiety or depression. This is anecdotal, of course, and doesn't mean it *can't* happen.

WHY PSYCHIATRIC BENEFITS COULD BE EXCLUDED FROM A POLICY

We'll cover medical underwriting in detail in Chapter Eight. In the meantime, I think it's worth a brief detour here as it relates to the psychiatric benefit.

A quick caveat that you already know but I want to remind you of—I'm not a psychiatrist or an underwriter or an actuary. I'm a disability insurance broker who specializes in providing disability insurance to physicians. As a result of this focus, I've walked through the medical underwriting process with literally thousands of physicians across the country. Our clients are from all over the world, which I love. The average age range is twenty-seven to thirty-five years old when they start working with us.

In our experience, from a medical screening standpoint, the psychiatric benefit is kind of like getting a loan from a bank— the bank will loan you the money you're requesting if you can prove you do not need the money, but if you really need the money, they will very likely refuse to loan it to you. The same is true for the psychiatric benefit—if you're applying for disability coverage and you've been treated recently or in the past two to five years for anxiety, the top companies will likely exclude the psychiatric benefit from the policy, at least initially. If, however, you have never needed counseling or medication for psychiatric issues, you can have this provision included in your policy without any problem (outside of the higher cost).

This is the rub. In our day and age, many people seek professional counseling. Many are on a stable dose of anxiety or ADHD medication. This is often a good thing. As a society, we're becoming more and more educated about mental health, emotional disorders, and stress-related illnesses.

This influx in treatment has its benefits, though not usually in the realm of disability coverage medical screening. In fact, it has the unfortunate side effect that if someone has ever been treated for psychiatric reasons, it can prevent them from receiving the psychiatric benefit. If you're taking an anxiety medication like Wellbutrin, then there's a good chance you could be excluded from the psychiatric benefit in your policy.

BUT INSURANCE COMPANIES ARE STARTING TO ADAPT

We've had clients who have gotten episodic counseling during medical school and take ADHD medication while they're studying and working twenty-four-hour shifts. Whether good or bad, it's often just the norm for them to work eighty hours a week. At times, it seems to me that physicians in training are basically ghosts, used and abused. They have no life. There are times when they may need the help of medication to stay focused, keep their energy, and not tap out.

For folks in this situation, things are looking up. The top insurance companies have started to recognize that if someone is taking a stable dose of Adderall, that doesn't always mean the person is unable to be insured with the best definitions. In the not-too-distant past (i.e., maybe ten to fifteen years ago), if a physician was applying for disability insurance while taking an ADHD medication, they might be a **total decline** even if they were otherwise healthy. Then, a few years later, the top companies would offer a person with this same scenario a modified policy with a five- or ten-year benefit period. Then, a few years after that, they started offering the applied-for benefit period to age sixty-five but would still exclude the future insurability option from the policy (i.e., in order to add coverage in the future, the insured had to redo all medical screening).

And now, as of this writing, the person in this same scenario (again, assuming they are otherwise healthy) can obtain the best definitions, the full benefit period, and the future insurability option. But the psychiatric benefit will still likely be excluded until the insured goes two to three years without medication and counseling (which may never happen and arguably should never happen...but that's a whole different discussion).

I'm a member of Strategic Coach, which is founded by Dan Sullivan, arguably the best coach of entrepreneurs and business owners the world has ever seen. In Strategic Coach, we talk about "the Gap and the Gain" and how vital it is to focus on the progress that's been made (i.e., the gain) instead of the long road we still have ahead (i.e., the gap). This is so true in terms of where we are with medical screening and the psychiatric benefit. It's important to remember that while it's not perfect, it's also never been this good.

As an FYI, I hear it's getting better still. If you're currently seeking treatment and taking anxiety medication and are otherwise very healthy, there could be a chance in the near future that a top disability insurance company will give you the two-year psychiatric benefit on your policy. Now, *that's* cutting edge! This is an evolving area that insurance companies and underwriters are still trying to figure out. They want to make sure they're keeping pace with where the evidence is showing they should be. But not surprisingly, companies that have the most to lose through that benefit are the slowest to change.

GETTING APPROVED BY STRICTER COMPANIES

If you have been excluded from receiving the psychiatric benefit on your policy, you may still be eligible to receive it in the future *if* you stop receiving treatment and taking medication for a certain number of years. To be clear: I am not advising anyone who needs psychiatric treatment to not receive the help they need. I am merely pointing out the guidelines currently in place.

If you have access to a guaranteed standard issue policy through your training institution, typically you will not be asked medical questions regarding treatment for anxiety. In that case, you will be able to have the psychiatric benefit, although it will likely be limited to two years in most cases.

I've also had situations where we've applied with multiple companies and pitted them against one another. Here's how it works: you disclose that you're applying with other companies and say you'll pick the best offer. This approach can be especially helpful if you're not sure exactly how people will treat you when they're looking at a compartmentalized version of your medical history.

"KICK THE CAN" IS A DANGEROUS GAME

When you're ready to get coverage, your underwriter may say, "Well, we need to exclude any psychiatric benefits. We can't pay you if you're disabled due to anxiety, depression, or addiction. We can cover everything else, but not psychiatric illnesses right now."

That's enough to upset someone. It might put such a bad taste in your mouth that you'll say, "Screw this. I'm not getting this coverage. I'm not concerned about being disabled. I'll just deal with it later."

Listen, I commend you for even reading about disability insurance; many of your colleagues are not even thinking about it. You deserve a major pat on the back for even exploring the subject: it is some major grownup stuff to do. But you have to follow through and get it. Dare I say—please don't revert to being a school kid. Don't take your ball and go home. I realize this can feel very unfair, but quitting can come back to hurt you *and* those you care about the most.

There is no "kicking the can down the road" with disability insurance. You really never know what could happen, and it's always best to get coverage when you're as healthy as possible. Even physicians can fall prey to thinking they're way healthier than they are. But neither you nor I have ever been Superman or Superwoman. In other words, we're all one bad day away from being uninsurable. *One* bad day.

CHAPTER SEVEN

SUPPLEMENTAL RIDERS

MOST INSURANCE COMPANIES HAVE EXTRA RIDERS THAT you can add to a disability policy. These companies build their disability contract for basically every different profession that they're willing to insure. Then they assign classifications for all the different occupations. Physicians are segmented into their own particular set of occupation classifications—and when you pick an occupation on their software, it automatically removes certain riders that are not available for this occupation classification, includes certain riders that they require, and highlights others that are potentially available.

So when you're comparing, say, four different top-tier disability contracts, knowing up from down is not easy. Based on my years of experience, there is a lot of confusion around supplemental riders. Some standard features are automatically built into your policy. However, there are other supplemental riders that I think we need to mention so you can have as full a picture as possible.

But before we look at those, let's turn our attention to an important built-in feature of a properly designed private specialty contract, the presumptive benefit. I bring this up here because it's auto-added to the top contracts, and so you'll be getting it in whatever you buy with the top companies.

THE PRESUMPTIVE BENEFIT

The **presumptive benefit** is a provision that all the top-tier specialty own occupation disability insurance companies include in their contracts. The presumptive benefit pays total disability benefits if certain events occur, such as a complete loss of hearing, total loss of sight in both eyes, loss of speech, or loss of use of any two limbs. With this benefit, if any of those events were to happen to you, your insurance company would *presume* (hence the name) that you're totally disabled and pay the full benefit, even if you were to keep working in your current occupation.

Usually, you don't pay any extra fee for this benefit—it's included automatically. However, each top specialty disability company defines it differently.

Also, it *doesn't* mean that you'd need to have, say, a complete loss of hearing in order to receive disability benefits altogether. It's an added benefit, not a restricted benefit. So, to be clear, if your hearing loss prevented you from being able to do your job anymore, and hearing loss was not otherwise excluded during the medical screening, your disability benefit would typically be activated.

Sticking with the example of hearing, let's say you did have a complete loss of hearing but continued to work in your occupation. The presumptive benefit would kick in and pay your full benefit even though you're still working and earning your income. One top specialty disability insurance company requires that your hearing loss be deemed *permanent* in order to activate their presumptive benefit. Other top companies would not require the hearing loss to be permanent. And one top company would also waive the elimination period and pay you immediately.

A few years ago, we had a client who had a stroke and temporarily lost the ability to walk. All of the top companies would have classified him as disabled because of the stroke. In his case, however, he happened to have a private specialty policy where the "loss of use of both legs" did not need to be permanent in order to activate the presumptive benefit. His contract also waived the normal ninety-day elimination period, so he started receiving his total disability benefit right away to compensate for his inability to use both legs.

Point is: while all the top companies include the presumptive benefit, they define it differently. It's worth looking into your provider's specific policy because there can be a lot of variation. Again, the devil is in the details with private specialty coverage.

THE ANNUAL INCREASE RIDER

The **annual increase rider (AIR)** is an optional rider that doesn't cost anything to include on the policy. The AIR automatically increases the base monthly benefit by a particular inflation factor every year. Usually, the increase is 4 percent per year without requiring further medical/financial underwriting (which we'll cover in the next chapter). When the benefit increases, the premium increases proportionally as well.

If included on your policy, the AIR is scheduled to increase annually for usually five years. It's assumed that you want this increased benefit (hence the term automatic). If you decide you *don't* want it, you have to notify the insurance company and/or your broker in writing.

When I launched my business and began working with clients, I believed that the annual increase rider was something that everybody should have, and I automatically included it and told clients it was on their policy.

But it became a pain point. When our clients purchase coverage, the premium is fixed unless they increase coverage. A number of clients interpreted the AIR increases to mean that the cost was increasing when they did not elect to increase coverage. So they would call and ask why their costs were going up. I'd have to explain, "You have this automatic increase rider, which increases your benefit by 4 percent, so it's also increasing your cost by 4 percent."

Then they would reply, "I don't want to do that. If I want to increase my policy, I'll do it through the future insurability option."

This reply made sense to me. Time is flying by. Even though it was the first policy anniversary, meaning a year had passed since they started, it likely felt like it was just a few months. It felt like every time they turned around they were getting dinged for a higher premium.

After fielding a number of requests from clients to cancel their rider, I realized that automatically including it was not the right approach. So now when it's discussed, I explain that (a) it can be good to include if you want to be sure your coverage "automatically" keeps pace with the higher cost of living and (b) most of our clients do not like it because it's a nuisance. Right or wrong, this approach has led our clients to make their own choice, and we don't get complaints about it much anymore.

THE STUDENT LOAN REPAYMENT RIDER

Something I've noticed over time is that when our trainee clients become attendings, often they come to realize that their higher income is nice but it doesn't go as far as they thought it would. They feel like they're being pinched from every angle— higher taxes, higher deductions to save for retirement, higher insurance costs, higher living expenses, etc.

Furthermore, even though their salary is very good, they don't feel flush because they still need to aggressively pay off school debts.

The clients who anticipate this upfront (i.e., while still in training) often explore including the **student loan repayment rider** on their private specialty policy. Not all insurance companies offer this, and it isn't approved in all fifty states. But where it's available, it's designed to pay an extra benefit, usually up to $2,500 a month, directly toward the repayment of your student loans. Each insurance company has its own cap for how long this benefit can be paid, usually up to ten or fifteen years. It covers the monthly payments for student loan debt while you're disabled, and it will pay as long as there is an outstanding balance (up to the previously mentioned ten- or fifteen-year maximum benefit period).

For example, if you have $5,000 a month of coverage, you can add a student loan rider that will pay an *additional* $2,500 a month directly to your student loan creditor. So, the loan payment is made while you receive the $5,000, which can now be used for expenses other than student loan debt. This rider adds about 10 to 15 percent to your monthly premium.

As an FYI, if you're thinking that the student loan repayment rider sounds like a cheap way to get an extra total disability benefit while you're disabled, think again. If you have this rider on your policy but no longer have student loans when you're disabled, the insurance company is not going to pay you the student loan rider amount. Rather, the money would go to any outstanding loan until it's paid off—and then it would go away.

THE RETIREMENT INCOME SUPPLEMENT RIDER

A couple of the top insurance companies have a **retirement income supplement rider,** or **retirement benefit rider,** that you can add to your policy. It's sometimes a rider you can add to a disability policy, and other times it's a separate policy.

Here's how it works. First, remember that if you become disabled, your policy will pay the stated monthly benefit in effect at the time of claim. If you have a retirement supplement rider, your provider sets aside this additional amount of the rider benefit into a trust. The funds are then allocated to interest-bearing accounts so that it (hopefully) grows toward your retirement. It's like putting money in an IRA or retirement plan to try to make up for lost retirement benefits that you'll miss out on due to being disabled. As benefits are paid, your contributions will be received income tax-free (as long as you did not deduct the premiums), and any gains will be taxable income.

The downside to these riders is that the definition of disability is usually more restrictive than the true specialty own occupation definition of disability. More specifically, in the retirement supplements we've seen, you would have to be totally disabled and could never earn income from another source while on claim. Also, if you're only partially disabled, typically it's not going to pay.

Lastly, the retirement income rider can also be relatively expensive when compared to other supplemental riders, like the student loan rider. It can add 40 percent or more to your disability insurance costs.

So, is it worth it? Generally, because of the definition limitations, we advise clients to avoid these and instead consider maximizing their specialty coverage benefit in order to be sure there's money available to continue funding retirement and other savings goals.

I know I've said this before, but it bears repeating now in relation to this section: so many of my clients qualify for $15,000 or $20,000 a month, but on occasion, a client will short-change themselves because they think they can live on $10,000 a month. "I'll take $10,000," they say. But down the road, they always wish they had that extra $5,000.

A mistake you want to avoid is basing your specialty coverage benefit on just your current fixed monthly expenses. This approach falls under the category of **"penny wise and dollar foolish"** for multiple reasons. Remember: expenses typically go *up* during a claim, not down. Even if you *can* live on $10,000 today, that additional $5,000 can really come in handy when you're trying to save for retirement. Also, it's wise to build in a buffer to be sure that some if not most of your important financial goals (children's college education, retirement, vacations) can still be funded.

As one final thought on this, the top disability insurance companies will *never* allow someone to "get rich" off of a claim. They have a financial formula they use to determine how much private specialty coverage you can purchase. If an underwriter tells you that you qualify financially for $15,000 a month, it's highly advisable to take their word for it that you'll need it if disabled.

LIFETIME BENEFITS (EXTINCT)

There used to be something called lifetime benefit periods. I'm only mentioning this briefly in case you've read about it on some website or blog. Insurance companies offered these lifetime benefit periods primarily back in the eighties and nineties. A couple of companies had them into the 2000s, and one even offered it for certain specialties until about 2015. If you could not perform your specialty, it was possible to have a lifetime benefit period included in your policy.

These are essentially impossible to purchase now. And even back toward the end of when they were available, insurance companies made it so expensive that hardly anyone would pay for it. It was as if they were hoping that no one would choose it as an option. This makes sense when you think about how long we're living now. Bottom line, it's very difficult to calculate the amount of money you should pay in premiums to an insurer to offset the risk of you living to 120.

THE CATASTROPHIC BENEFIT

The **catastrophic benefit** pays an additional monthly benefit if you cannot perform two of the six activities of daily living (ADLs). As you may already know (but so they're handy), the ADLs are:

1. Dressing

2. Toileting

3. Transferring

4. Continence

5. Eating

6. Bathing

If you're unable to perform at least two of these, the catastrophic benefit will activate to pay you the additional benefit (which is selected at the time you purchase your specialty disability policy). This is essentially long-term care insurance until age sixty-five or whatever benefit period is on your policy. Depending on the insurance company, this rider usually adds 10 to 15 percent to your overall premium.

As you might expect, the threshold to engage this benefit is high. As of this writing, we've not had any clients claim this benefit. Nor have I talked with colleagues who have. For what it's worth, most of our clients do not currently opt for including this rider. All that said, the catastrophic benefit can be attractive for people who want to be extra cautious. In other words, they want to be sure that additional benefits will be paid to offset the higher cost of care that a catastrophic event usually involves.

Sorry if you're hoping I would just tell you to do it or not do it. Ultimately, it's a personal call regarding how much risk you want to self-insure or pass along to the insurance company.

ARE ALL THESE RIDERS NECESSARY?

If you're like most physicians, when you're shopping for disability coverage, ultimately you're looking at cost. That's just a business reality: cost matters. People are generally looking for the best deal. I'm sensitive to that. And so I don't include fluff riders on policies without first talking to my clients—about the monthly costs as well as the benefits.

The catastrophic rider, for example, is one that doesn't usually make the cut. Now, if a client brings it up and wants it, I'm fine with adding it. But most of our clients don't want it. I'm not exactly sure why they tend to see it this way, but once they really understand it, they just don't feel compelled to pay the extra cost.

Some insurance professionals may say that I'm making a mistake by not pushing it harder. They argue that I have a responsibility to try to talk you into spending an extra 10 or 15 percent because of that one-off chance that you're going to be a quadriplegic, or in a vegetative state, and you'll need the catastrophic benefit to afford to live until you're sixty-five and beyond.

I understand this viewpoint. But this could be the case with every rider if you look at it in a vacuum. It's like a dermatologist having multiple approaches to advising patients to avoid skin cancer, but the patient is limited in (a) their ability to do "all of the above" and (b) how much they really care about it at this current moment. We're human, so we cannot cover every single scenario all the time.

There are three hills I am willing to die on, and I've already talked about these earlier in the book (Chapter Zero and Chapter One). They are the true specialty own occupation definition of disability, the residual benefit, and the recovery benefit. Beyond this, I'm not going to push someone to add things that they don't want.

CHAPTER EIGHT

MEDICAL UNDERWRITING

MEDICAL UNDERWRITING IS OFTEN OVERLOOKED AS AN easy step by young and healthy-ish physician trainees. They're so busy working sixty to eighty hours per week, they "kick the can down the road," figuring they'll get to it later. This approach works...until it doesn't.

Take the stories of Tim and Paul: both were young physicians in residency, and both were in good health overall but had recently encountered medical issues.

Tim had developed an eye disease called keratoconus, which means his cornea had become cone-shaped. Before this happened, he and I had been emailing for a while about disability insurance options. Now, after receiving the diagnosis, he had finally decided it was time to buy. "I can still get coverage, right?" he asked. I explained to him that unfortunately, as I had mentioned in our prior communications, this type of private own occupation disability coverage for physicians requires medical underwriting approval. Because keratoconus is a lifelong illness, his eyes would likely be permanently excluded from his private coverage.

Paul was in the same boat. He had been researching disability insurance for a while, and I had been referred to him by someone he trusted. But for whatever reason, he could just never pull the trigger. Doctors are busy, and Paul was putting in eighty hours a week. One day, he finally reached out to me and said, "Hey, Billy, I'm ready to do this." But then he added, "I do have a question, though...I have to have surgery on my ears in four weeks. Will this affect my ability to get coverage?" He went on to tell me all about the operation. It wasn't the most serious thing in the world, but it wasn't a minor procedure. So I gave him the bad news: he was essentially uninsurable until this was all over and he had fully recovered, meaning back at work for at least thirty days with no complications. Even at that point, it was likely his insurance policy would exclude his ears for at least the first few years. Depending on the outcome of the surgery, it might even have to be a permanent exclusion.

I bring up these examples as cautionary tales. Assuming you are still healthy and haven't been disabled, you should have no problem obtaining coverage (subject, of course, to whatever definitions and discounts are in place at the time). But *until* you decide to buy, all bets are off.

So please don't let what happened to Tim and Paul happen to you. Again, physicians are busy and especially so when they're still in training. They're also not making much money at this stage in their career. I know there are real issues involved that can legitimately prevent someone from making a significant purchase like disability insurance. And of course, we've all been taught to shop around and not swing at the first pitch. But as you saw in these examples, holding off too long can be very risky.

The best time to get your private specialty own occupation disability insurance is when you think you need it least.

When you seem bulletproof, when you feel like you're Superman or Wonder Woman, *that's* when you should do it. You'll get the best policy at the lowest rate.

Don't wait until it's too late and you realize you're not the superhero you thought.

WHAT IS MEDICAL UNDERWRITING

The top disability insurance companies like to offer enticing discounts to young, healthy physicians who they know are going to be paying premiums hopefully for a long, long time. In theory, this is a very profitable stream of income for these companies. But it's also great for you, the person being insured—because you're getting the best coverage possible at the lowest rate possible.

It's hard to see what a good deal it is until you actually need the insurance. Say you pay a premium for twenty or twenty-five years. You may think you're wasting your money. But if you're disabled in the twenty-first year and receive a claim check for even less than one year, you win financially. So it doesn't take many claims to wipe out an insurance provider's profitability entirely.

Of course, insurance companies try to better their odds, and that's where medical underwriting comes in. **Medical underwriting** (sometimes called medical screening) occurs when insurance companies medically evaluate potential policyholders before they issue a policy. They want to know as much as possible about the applicant upfront so that they can (hopefully) offer coverage to healthy applicants, exclude pre-existing conditions where possible, and also unfortunately deny coverage to people who are not medically qualified. It is discriminatory by nature. While it may sound harsh, it's also what enables the largest number of people to get the best level of coverage.

Underwriters need to determine whether someone's prior medical conditions and health history fit within the parameters for offering the best coverage. Inevitably, some applicants get denied. But the vast majority are accepted, and, as intimidating as the process may seem, it's important to remember that statistically speaking you're unlikely to be declined completely.

Still, you should know and understand this basic reality of how insurance companies work. This is another reason that it matters who your agent/broker is. If they specialize in disability insurance particularly for physicians, navigating this process can go much smoother.

THE APPLICATION PROCESS: UNDERWRITING FROM THE CONSUMER STANDPOINT

If a physician is in training, still young and healthy, when they begin the medical underwriting process, things are usually less nerve-wracking. Generally, there's no question about whether or not the insurance company will accept them—they are a shoo-in (unless there's a hiccup like a psychiatric component, which we covered in Chapter Six).

The top disability companies have significantly streamlined the underwriting process to where it's all electronic and over the phone. In most cases, the insurance physical is waived for trainees and is never required in the future either. All of which is to say that as it stands today, medical underwriting has never been easier for trainees.

As an FYI, some residency programs at times get insurance companies to offer something called guaranteed standard issue insurance, which means you can get disability coverage without medical underwriting. There are usually just a few "gatekeeper" questions. In our experience, these programs tend (as one might expect) to attract people who already know they may be uninsurable. This is as it should be, right? But because of the strong potential for "adverse selection" (i.e., more unhealthy people opting in than healthy people), these policies often have added restrictions in the definitions, coverage amounts, or both. If you have a significant medical history, guaranteed standard issue insurance is an alternative you should seek out. If you're on the healthier side (we'll call it "healthy-ish"), then going the streamlined medical screening route can be helpful to avoid any policy restriction pitfalls, seen or unseen. Whichever way you go, just be sure you understand the details in writing before applying.

If you're healthy-ish and going through the medical screening process, in most cases you'll just need to e-sign a completed application and hop on a phone call or click an online link from the underwriter to answer about twenty to twenty-five medical questions. As part of the application, you also e-sign a HIPAA form consenting to the release of your medical records should the underwriter need to review them. In my experience with the underwriters at top companies (I cannot speak for companies outside the handful that offer the top-tier contracts), they are not going on scavenger hunts looking at records for a reason to deny coverage. Sometimes they just need to verify details about past medical conditions, medications, treatment, etc.

The underwriter will also do a script check. This is an important point to understand. Underwriters are going to find out what medicines you've been prescribed. So just be upfront about it. If you tell the underwriter on the phone interview, for example, that you've never been treated for anxiety, but they look it up and see that you had a prescription for anti-anxiety medications that was filled six months ago, they're going to want you to explain what's up!

An important word of caution: "self-prescribing" medications is a problem. Getting a physician friend or colleague to write you a script without a chart (i.e., without an office visit or at least a note documenting why you're being treated with the medication) is also a problem.

I'm not referring to a prescription for a topical ointment to treat a skin rash you got while camping over the weekend. I'm referring to writing yourself, or having a friend write for you, a script for Adderall or a sleep aid to get through a tough stretch during residency. This is risky business in many worlds, including the disability insurance underwriting world.

And it can cause an otherwise healthy person to have exclusions added to their policy or, in some cases, be declined completely.

DISABILITY INSURANCE FOR PHYSICIANS

It's not that the underwriter thinks you're a criminal. It's that insurance companies are excellent at understanding human nature. They pay actuaries a lot of money to price insurance products as accurately as possible. These actuaries study volumes of statistical analyses of how people who have certain characteristics increase or decrease their chances of becoming disabled. And believe it or not, apparently physicians who self-prescribe are significantly higher risks than people who do not.

You might be surprised to learn how often I've had to help clients navigate these situations. It can get muddy, and it's so unnecessary. Underwriters know you're not Superman or Superwoman. We all have times when we need some kind of help. And this can be especially true for physicians while in medical school, residency, and/or fellowship. The underwriters at these top specialty disability insurance companies know this. It's okay to get the help you need, especially when it's a situational thing that gets better over time. Just be sure it's all documented and communicated accurately.

What you or I may assume is not a big deal may or may not actually be so. As they say, the numbers don't lie. And the numbers are the numbers, whether you know about it beforehand or not. So, bottom line, just be sure there is a chart to support the need—permanent or temporary/situational—for prescription medications. Then the medical screening process is likely to go much smoother.

Regarding the insurance physical mentioned earlier, if you start at a trainee initial benefit of \$5,000 or \$6,000 per month, the top companies will waive the physical (which involves a nurse visit for blood and urine samples, height/weight measurements, medical questions, and usually blood pressure reading). Also, if you purchase at the time you're graduating with a signed employment contract, some companies will let you start at \$10,000 a month of coverage or even higher without the physical. This can change over time.

Again, if you're healthy-ish, you'll get the best coverage and the largest discount. You're never going to get a better deal than when you're in residency or fellowship. At any juncture later in your career as an attending, you should expect to pay more—perhaps much more.

Clearly, it's ideal to get coverage while you're still young. But if that ship has sailed for you, there's nothing you can do—just make sure you take action before it's too late. The important thing is that your coverage is in place *before* your disability occurs.

Which brings me to an important point...

INDIVIDUAL VS. GROUP DISABILITY INSURANCE

There are several large medical associations (I'll refrain from naming names here) that have policies they promote as specialty-specific, portable private coverage. But it's actually a *group certificate.* It breaks my heart to know that probably no one buying this junk (stating it mildly) understands the downside of having a group certificate as opposed to an individual policy. This is crucial information for anyone looking into disability insurance.

So, what *is* the difference between the two?

An **individual policy** is a policy where the individual being insured calls all the shots once the policy is issued. *You* decide how long you want to keep it and when you're going to terminate it. If it's structured right, the insurance company can never change the definitions on you. Your premium is fixed for life. Your policy can never be canceled or terminated unless you, the individual, decide to.

With a **group policy**, it's exactly the opposite. The insurance company owns the policy by default and calls all the shots. If they start to not like the claims they're getting, or they simply decide these policies are not "on mission" for them as a company, they can actually terminate the group policy altogether. Or they can increase the rate. They can also change the definitions. Or, again, they can just walk away.

It's bad news for the physician who is counting on this to be their personal coverage. You could be a forty-five-year-old physician who got your policy when you were thirty, and now, fifteen years later, you're a type 2 diabetic and getting a letter that says, essentially, "Thirty days from now, you won't have a policy."

Don't let that happen to you.

LIFE INSURANCE VS. DISABILITY INSURANCE UNDERWRITING

As you might expect with life insurance, life *expectancy* plays a big role. Life insurance underwriters are looking at conditions and health factors that impact your longevity from a *life* standpoint.

But the underwriting department for disability insurance is not the same as the one for life insurance. What matters to disability underwriters is the risk that something will happen to you that doesn't *kill* you but does keep you from working.

The underwriting, or screening, processes are very different too. The underwriters are trained differently. Life underwriters and disability underwriters are not even in the same department of the insurance company. At least in my experience, they're like two separate sides of the insurance business.

I've seen situations where, from a disability standpoint, someone is almost uninsurable, but when it comes to *life* insurance they somehow manage to get the best rate. For example, one client of mine had severe back problems, significant enough that two insurers rejected him outright for disability insurance. Apparently, though, because the back issues were not a factor in his life expectancy, he was able to get a great rate for life insurance.

Whereas disability underwriters care about back pain (and life insurance underwriters often don't), disability underwriters *don't* care as much about things like taking cholesterol medication. They're much more interested in your lifestyle and chronic conditions. They want to know if you've had knee surgery, wrist problems, psychiatric issues, and so on. That's why they'll ask questions like: "Do you miss any work because of sicknesses or depression?"

Answering yes to something like that could understandably lead a disability underwriter to believe it's more likely the company will be on the hook for a claim later on—and they know that with this private specialty occupation coverage, if an illness or injury keeps you from working, they'll be paying a lot of money perhaps for a very long time. Of course, ideally they prefer to take on policyholders who will *make* the company money, not *cost* the company money. For better or worse, insurance is a business, and these are business decisions.

HOW COVID IS CHANGING UNDERWRITING

Medical screening has continued to evolve in recent years—thanks, in large part, to COVID-19. One silver lining of the pandemic is that it forced insurance companies to further adapt and change the way they perform their medical screenings. Nowadays, the process has never been easier.

In 2020 and beyond, prospective insurance applicants were, of course, concerned about contracting COVID and preferred not having nurses coming into their homes. Nurses themselves were also concerned. During the height of quarantine, going into a stranger's house or apartment was something to avoid if at all possible. And even now, at the time of this writing, a lot of people still don't want to have unnecessary interactions if they don't have to.

In terms of disability insurance, what we've seen over the past couple of years is that prospective customers will pass on buying insurance altogether if it means having to get a physical and risk contracting COVID.

Facing this new reality, the insurance world has continued to change in regard to underwriting. Before COVID, the top disability insurance companies were already doing the vast majority of their medical screening electronically and over the phone, particularly for trainees. COVID appears to have cemented this as the new normal and not just experimental.

Now, to be clear, you're still being medically underwritten. It's just all remote. The underwriter can still retrieve your medical records if needed. But now they also recognize that they don't necessarily need things like urinalysis, blood profile, or EKG to determine if you're healthy-ish.

One top disability insurance company even came out recently and said, "When you're graduating and becoming an attending, you can purchase any amount up to $20,000 per month *without a physical*." That's never been done before in my recollection. Usually, if you wanted more than $5,000 per month, or certainly more than $7,500 per month, you would have to do the physical.

TIMING MATTERS

Earlier in this chapter, we talked about how, even with all the different factors being considered, you're unlikely to get rejected for coverage. That said, it *does* happen. We also see scenarios where clients are approved but exclusions are added for pre-existing conditions.

What if something like this happens to you? First of all, don't freak out. **And don't give up.** Just because you were offered a modified contract doesn't mean it's forever. Or just because you were turned down by one company doesn't mean you can't get coverage somewhere else. And it certainly doesn't automatically mean that you'll *never* be able to get coverage whatsoever. But these situations do make it that much more important that you have an expert broker who specializes in disability coverage to help you.

Remember: insurance companies are not looking for perfect humans. It may seem like that sometimes, based on your experience with the underwriting process. But in reality, insurers understand that people have prior surgeries and conditions. If you have a pre-existing condition, yes, it can make the process more complicated but not impossible. Keep in mind that **the top disability insurance companies try to isolate the pre-existing condition while still offering you coverage for everything else.**

One company might offer a reduced benefit period. For example, they could offer a five-year or ten-year benefit period per disability. Another top company might say, "We can offer a benefit period to age sixty-five." You're the same person, same medical history, but you get two different offers. Believe it or not, while very similar in most regards, the top disability companies view the risk world differently. One company's actuaries are more conservative than another company's actuaries. Also, underwriters can at times be more aggressive during medical underwriting than other underwriters.

A few years back, an interventional radiologist called me about his existing private own occupation policy with one of the top insurers. He has a heart condition that he was diagnosed with back when he was only ten years old. He never had to get any treatment, but he still has the diagnosis on his medical record. He gets it checked every couple years, but he doesn't really need to do anything beyond that. His doctor said, "When you're seventy or eighty, you might need to have a valve replaced or something. In the meantime, there's nothing you need to do."

His insurance company offered him a ten-year benefit period. He's forty years old. That means if he gets disabled today, they'll pay him until he's fifty, and then he's done. So he asked me, "Is it worth it for me to shop this offer? Can you help me get a benefit period to age sixty-five? Because if you can, I'm not married to this particular company."

I said, "Email me a snapshot of your situation and history. I'll discuss informally with the three other current top-tier companies." The underwriters said, "No way we can beat this. He should not have even gotten the offer he has. We cannot do better." So I told him to keep what he had and view it as gold— and to not let anyone *ever* tell him to get rid of it.

There have been times when I've gotten people approved that were long shots and medically shouldn't have been approved. In these cases, my team and I were successful because (a) we happened to make our ask at the right time, (b) we pushed the underwriter, and (c) the insurance company made a business decision. We hit a home run because the insurance company decided it was worth the risk to them at that particular point.

Unfortunately, there's no way to fully predict this kind of thing ahead of time. When potentially significant medical histories are involved, you just have to try your best, case by case. And I'll say it again, this is why it's essential—vital even—to work with a broker who specializes in disability insurance for physicians. Navigating this process takes an expert if you want the best shot at the best coverage.

CHAPTER NINE

CONTRACTS

WHEN IT COMES TO DISABILITY INSURANCE CONTRACTS, the devil is in the details. In fact, when you file a claim, the details are *everything*. Don't expect the claims department to ask what your broker told you or what *you* think your coverage entails. All they're going to do is pull out your contract and read it.

What about you? Have *you* read through your contract? Do you know what it says?

As you are well aware by now, I work with physicians, who are smart people. But they still often have a tough time fully grasping the confusing language in insurance contracts. It's understandable: the jargon *is* confusing, and the documents can be very tedious to read through. Not only that, but physicians have to deal with incredibly complicated medical situations every day. The last thing they probably want to do during their downtime is delve into a disability insurance contract.

Nonetheless, I urge you to do exactly that. When you do, it's important to remember—highlight, save a note, whatever it takes—the pages of the vital terms to reference in the future.

Don't get me wrong: as a broker, it's my job to explain these things to clients and answer their questions, and of course I love helping them. This is why it's so important to have a broker you can trust, who will pay special attention to the details. But unfortunately, there are many brokers out there who will gloss over these items, telling you things like, "Don't worry about that" and "It's no big deal."

I've actually come across some agents who don't even send the full policy to their clients at all, instead wanting their clients to contact them if they ever want to know anything about their policy. This may seem at first like good customer service, but it isn't. It's dangerous for the policyholder. As I mentioned earlier, at claim time, what your agent told you your policy said is not what will determine whether or not you get paid. The written contract is everything. So you need to have a full copy stored with your other important papers.

At the time of claim, the only thing that will matter is what the contract says.

BUT WHY IS THE CONTRACT SO LONG?

Recently, a client of mine, an oncologist, asked me to send him a copy of his policy and summarize the key points. I gladly obliged and emailed him the full fifty-one-page PDF doc. Light reading, right? I also gave him a summary of the pages where the key definitions and riders were located in the contract.

But there's no getting around the fact that these contracts seem like monsters. They include everything from a definition section to the clauses that determine exceptions (act of war, intentional self-inflicted injury, etc.) to the supplemental riders and benefits. Just the prospect of reading through the whole thing can be understandably daunting, and then when you actually dive in, I can't lie, it's probably even more boring than you imagined! But there are details throughout that are incredibly important.

In particular, I directed the oncologist client to the page where he could find details related to the specialty own occupation definition of disability. Each insurance company has multiple versions of their disability contract, including several different disability definitions for various occupations. Plumbers, for example, don't have access to the same definitions that a surgeon does. That's not because one industry is better or worse than another. But the way insurance operates, an actuary has to compile data and assign risk categories to different occupations. If your occupation is more risky, like carpentry or cleaning windows on skyscrapers, the definitions they offer are different than if you're in a less risky occupation like accounting. The policies are built around industry-specific risks.

Another important section of these contracts is the part that details enhanced residual benefits. This section usually contains a formula for how the provider calculates partial disability benefits and recovery benefits.

Again, even if you have a solid broker who can explain your contract to you, I advise you to read through it yourself, note the key pages, and also ask your broker questions. **Do not rely solely on someone else to tell you about your policy.**

REQUEST A COPY OF YOUR POLICY IN FULL

I had a client situation with a New Mexico–based neurologist who had a policy with a large insurance company. He reached out to me because he had done some research and had also been told by some colleagues that his was not a "true" own occupation policy. They said he ought to look instead at one of the top own occupation companies.

They were right. The particular insurance company that he had been using is highly rated, but their contract is sub-par from a definition standpoint. To compare: if the contracts I broker with clients are "A-plus," this insurance company's would be, at best, a "C." But, of course, their in-house captive agents talk about their contract as if it's "A-plus." Right off the bat, I had a bad feeling. But I agreed to take a look. I asked the neurologist to send me his current policy.

That's when he told me he didn't have it because the agent said his company usually doesn't send the actual policy to clients. They just send a summary.

A red flag if I ever saw one.

Summaries may seem useful because they use all the appropriate buzz words—but without definitions compiled in a contract, summaries are meaningless. They can use phrases like "specialty specific" or "specialty occupation" all they want, but if they don't explicitly define these terms, then you're left having to guess or assume what they mean. And in my experience, it seems as if they're *hoping* you infer wrongly. It's a sleazy way to do business.

With this company, to request a copy of the full policy, you have to go through the agent, which sends off alarm bells for them. They wonder, *Why do you need it, and what are you looking for?* and quickly go into defense mode. (At least that's my perception: I've never actually worked for them, nor would I want to. However, I've spent a lot of time correcting issues that certain insurance agents and companies allow to exist in the marketplace.)

In the case of the neurologist, what happened next was I gave him the results of my own analysis. He then called the existing policy agent, who, of course, told him I had it all wrong. So, I gave my client the hard truth: if he were to ever get disabled, it wouldn't matter what his agent told him.

The contract is all that matters.

I sent him the new contract *that I recommended* in its entirety, all forty-six pages, and suggested he have the other agent look it over, since it was fair game. My idea was that the agent could then tell him (and me, by proxy) where it failed to measure up. He could highlight the phrases and cite the page numbers. If I was wrong, he'd have me exposed completely. I also suggested the other agent send him (and me, again by proxy) a copy of *his* entire contract for my review and feedback.

The neurologist thought it was a great idea and agreed to do it.

Problem was, he couldn't get his agent to give him a copy of the policy.

The neurologist eventually went with the policy that I proposed. He told me he appreciated how I operated. He had been a long-time client of the other agent, had purchased life insurance from him, and had even used him for investments. But now he was just so put off that this agent wouldn't show him the actual policy. And I believe he was right to trust his intuition.

CONTRACTS I KNOW BY HEART

If you want to avoid this type of situation altogether, you might want an expert's input on which companies are the best to work with—and specifically, which ones have the best contracts. When clients (or readers, in this case) ask me which contract I would choose if I was in their situation, I take it very seriously because I know how much trust that takes.

There are a few insurance companies that are well known yet have subpar contracts. Yet people can still gravitate toward them due to the fact that they're household names. It's psychology; we can't help it. But because these companies have some major gaps in their contracts, I don't work with them. I don't want a single client of mine to be stuck with their contract.

At the time of this writing, there are, based on contract strength and overall company financial soundness, only four top-tier specialty own occupation disability insurance contracts. If you want them named, reach out to me directly or check out my blog with podcasts about each: https://www.ownoccdisability. com/blog.

Of these four, there are some secondary differences that tend to draw people to one over another, depending on their specific situation. That said, based on our experience, it's totally okay to just pick the cheapest of the four if that's your main concern, as long as it has the key riders and benefits on it. You're not making a mistake if you're choosing from these top contracts.

That's why our clients pick from this small list. They're the best of the best, and nothing else comes close. Whichever one our clients choose, they're going to be well cared for.

BEWARE OF COMPANY AND ASSOCIATION BRANDING

Several well-known (you've probably heard of them) insurance companies and associations like to use medical and specialty jargon to convince physicians—and even some agents—that they're in good hands. And when you call up a big association like this to talk to them about the disability policy they sponsor, unfortunately, you'll usually be speaking with a customer service representative who makes, give or take, $15 per hour. They'll simply tell you what *they* have been told, like reading a script. Keep in mind that this person has likely received minimal training and probably never actually worked in the insurance field. Or, if they have, they learned just enough to make them dangerous.

To be clear, I'm not suggesting that customer service reps on the other end of 1-800 numbers are evil people who wake up and say, "I'm going to deliberately mislead customers today." But they *do* appear to blindly trust that because they've been told it's a good policy they're selling, it must *be* a good policy— and so they have no qualms about recommending it to people who call them.

More specifically, the conversations with insurance company reps often go something like this: you ask them if a policy includes such-and-such benefits, and they just say yes and hope you don't have any follow-up questions. Sometimes they literally have no clue what the benefit in question even *is*. Either way, it's a case of the uninformed talking to the uninformed.

Even with agents associated with large insurance companies, many of them have drunk so much of the corporate Kool-Aid that they sell products they've never thoroughly examined or vetted. They are essentially no different than their clients, searching Google for information even though *they* are supposed to be the experts!

I'm not trying to be harsh. I like to think the best of people. But these insurance companies, associations, and agents who muddy the waters—with their weak contracts and lack of knowledge—make it difficult for the very people they're supposed to help. They make the public less likely to trust *any* company or broker.

It's one of the reasons I choose to be independent. No insurance company pays my rent, my electric bill, or anything other than a commission when I connect a client with one of their policies. (By the way, the commission is paid even if a policyholder wants to go directly, so it should at least go to someone who knows what they're doing.) And I only work with a handful of companies that I trust and know with certainty have solid contracts.

CHAPTER TEN

CHARACTERISTICS OF A GOOD BROKER

When I say the word "blue," chances are you have a specific shade that instinctively comes to mind, just as I have a shade of blue that comes to my mind. And the amazing thing is that I could very well be imagining a color that's wildly different than yours. Maybe you are seeing a Carolina (sky) blue, whereas I am thinking of a Duke (dark) blue.

Sticking with this example, let's say you and I are business partners and decide to paint our office. We discuss different options for colors and agree ultimately on blue. Then, you offer to paint the whole thing yourself while I am away on a business trip. *What a great idea*, I think to myself. *I can just come back from the trip and the office will be painted—perfect! I trust you to handle it.* But when I come back, the look of the office is not at all what I expect. The shade of blue is *very* different from what I had in mind.

How could we have avoided this unfortunate situation? First, we have to look at how we got here.

From the beginning, we had been saying the same word and assuming we were on the same page. We'd both been imagining the future office and believing our respective visions were in alignment. But in the end—after the paintbrush met the wall and I saw what color you used—we realized we were way off. Our definitions of blue were miles apart, even though, yes, we'd been using the same exact language the whole time.

At this point, you're probably wondering: *Billy, why all this talk about the color blue?*

Within my niche market of disability insurance for physicians, there can be a lot of lingo that sounds the same, or at least very similar, but often means dramatically different things. So, it's like a significant percentage of insurance people and physicians alike go around saying the word "blue" and, in reality, they are not even close to being on the same page.

As an example, first and foremost is the long, wordy term I utilize in describing the best definition of disability: "private specialty own occupation." When I say this term in this book and with our clients, I mean something very specific. In particular, I mean that if an illness or injury prevents you from performing the material duties of your specialty occupation (as defined by treatment/procedural codes), then you're considered totally disabled, regardless of any income you earn doing a different occupation (whether in medicine or outside of medicine).

But when an insurance company, professional association, or employer uses similar phrasing (such as "specialty specific" or "medical specialty" or any number of other such catch-phrases), they can and usually do mean something very different. As explored in Chapter Two, how their contract defines total disability is *not* how the top specialty disability contracts define it. So while they may use the same terms, the *meaning* is completely different.

It's difficult to understate the difference. As also discussed earlier, the vast majority of disabilities are *not* catastrophic. In numerous policies outside the top specialty own occupation contracts, even if you cannot continue working in your specialty, you might never collect benefits from these policies. That's because the contract language is worded so as to make it difficult to meet their definition of disability.

I've seen and heard about this more than I wish—people who don't realize until it's too late that they're not actually speaking the same language as their provider. Again, the devil is in the details, and **my job is to make sure my clients get the same shade of blue they think they're getting.**

That's why, again, it's so important to find not just any broker, but the *right* one. How can you tell if your broker fits the bill?

First, if your broker is a good one, they should be making sure you understand certain key points and are speaking the same language.

Specifically, here are some of the important points that a good broker will cover:

THE THREE NON-NEGOTIABLES

When you and your broker discuss how your own occupation policy should be designed, it should contain all three of these: the **specialty own occupation definition of disability**, the **long-term residual benefit**, and the **long-term recovery benefit**.

Defined in detail in Chapter One, these are the three non-negotiables of a solid disability policy. If one or more of these are not present, keep looking.

It's the three-legged stool that any well-designed policy stands on. Without all three legs, you cannot sit on it. If one or more are missing, it's not adequate.

Typically the most overlooked, the long-term recovery benefit is the most important feature to a good policy that most people—even insurance agents—have never heard of. If you're disabled and return to work, but when you return, your income does not "recover" to the pre-disability level, the recovery benefit would continue to pay you partial benefits. This is a vital benefit. With the current pay structure for most physicians being heavy on bonuses for productivity, this feature has never been more important.

A good broker will want to make sure you know you have all three of the non-negotiables. And even if you forget they are included (which will likely happen), they'll be happy to remind you how and why each is so crucial.

ASSUMPTIONS YOU WILL NEED TO MAKE

As we've covered earlier, part of the process of securing your disability insurance involves choosing **the elimination period**. Typically the options are either ninety days or 180 days. Clients often ask me, "Which one should I do? Which one is better?"

My answer is usually, "Good question, as the difference is important. Ultimately, it's a personal call based on which assumption you want to make." The first assumption is that you *do* become disabled. In this case, you'll want a shorter elimination period. Six months is a long time to wait when you're newly disabled due to an illness or an injury and with no income coming in. It's usually a scary time, a sobering time. You start to see how your expenses for medical care and medications and PT are piling up. Health insurance will cover some but usually not all of it. Under this assumption, you'll want the ninety-day elimination period.

The second assumption is that you *don't* become disabled. Under this assumption, you'll see the higher cost of the shorter elimination period as wasted money. You'll rather have the longer 180-day elimination period and pocket the difference in cost savings.

The decision is yours. It's your broker's job to be sure you understand the difference.

Clients also ask me, "Should I pay for the COLA (Cost of Living Adjustment) rider?" Again, my answer, essentially, is that it depends on which assumption you want to make. The first assumption is that you become disabled at an earlier age and are disabled for an extended period (say ten years or longer). In this case, you'd likely be glad you paid the extra premium to have the COLA rider included.

Keep in mind too that inflation is real and about as guaranteed to occur as death and taxes (not quite equal to those but close). It's pretty much a given that in ten years $5,000 or $20,000 a month will not go as far as it does now. Having the COLA rider helps offset this reality.

If, however, you are operating under the second assumption—which is that you either do not become disabled or only become disabled for a short period of time—the COLA rider is not helpful. I said it once and I'll say it again: your broker's responsibility is to clearly communicate the differences. Then the final decision is yours.

UNDERSTANDING THE TERMS "NON-CANCELABLE" AND "GUARANTEED RENEWABLE"

The insurance industry is known for creating unnecessary confusion by mislabeling certain terms. One we covered earlier in the book is underwriters and insurance insiders referring to the psychiatric benefit as the "mental/nervous" benefit.

Another one is understanding the difference between *non-cancelable* and *guaranteed renewable*. As covered in Chapter Three, these terms can scare clients into thinking they cannot ever cancel their own policy and/or it somehow can be terminated or changed by the company at any time without notice.

A good broker will make sure you understand both of these terms, whether you're initially signing up for coverage or need clarification when you increase coverage in the future.

"Non-cancelable" (also known as "non-cancelable *and* guaranteed renewable") means that your policy can never be canceled by the company (you can cancel anytime, they cannot), the contract terms can never change, and the rate can never be increased.

"Guaranteed renewable" (also known as "guaranteed renewable-only"), on the other hand, means that your policy can never be canceled by the company, the contract terms can never change, but your rate *can* be increased by state and

115

occupation classification. The benefit of this option is that the premium is about 15 percent less than the non-cancelable premium.

Not all of the top disability insurance companies offer the *guaranteed renewable-only* option. If the company you want does offer this, it's worth exploring whether or not the company has a clean track record. For example, one of the current top disability companies offers this option, and in the sixty or so years they've been selling policies to the public, they've never once raised their rates on existing policyholders. That's a solid track record.

Why would a top disability company choose not to raise its rates on you even though it has the right to? It's because the biggest issue for the insurance company raising rates, and what most people don't think about, is the real-world impact of adverse selection. This one issue—adverse selection—dogs insurance companies in virtually everything they do. Remember, insurance policies are not mortgages; you do not have to keep the policy any longer than you want to keep it. The insurance company cannot walk away, but you can walk away anytime. So if the insurance company raises the rate for some or all guaranteed renewable policies, the healthy-ish policyholders are going to look for a better option and jump ship.

At the same time, the less healthy are going to stay put and pay the higher rate because they do not have a better option besides self-insuring. So after raising, in the final analysis, the insurance company ends up with a less healthy policyholder population. In other words, they just made their problem even worse than before they did the increase. This is adverse selection: the unintended consequences of making a current/new decision to fix a past decision.

Smart people like to know their options. A good number of our clients like the opportunity to save an additional 15 percent or so on their rate, and they're okay with the slightly higher risk with a solid company in order to get it. Others don't want to give any insurance company a chance to jack up their rate, which I completely understand. Both are right in their own way. And either option is fine. A good broker just wants to be sure you know the choice is there.

THE WISDOM OF ACCEPTING A MODIFIED CONTRACT BECAUSE OF MEDICAL HISTORY

As covered in Chapter Seven, complications from medical underwriting is something we occasionally have to discuss with our clients. Good brokers know how to navigate this well.

A client will ask me, for example, "If I can only get a policy with a five- or ten-year benefit period because of health reasons, should I still get it? Is it worth it if I don't have a benefit period until age sixty-five?"

This is a good and reasonable question. My answer is that unless there is a better option (and usually there is not), it's worth it. The average disability claim for a professional, healthy-ish male or female is 82 months (according to the CDA). Over 60 percent of disability claims are two years or less. From a big-picture perspective, it's definitely beneficial to have a five- or ten-year benefit period.

Furthermore, typically a policy modified with a shorter benefit period will also have a lower corresponding premium, compared to policies with a benefit period to age sixty-five or seventy.

While it's obviously not as good as you might hope, it's important to not throw the baby out with the bathwater. You and your family relying solely on an employer group LTD policy and/or self-insuring is a brutal reality if a disability occurs. As I regularly tell physicians who are making these types of significant decisions, "It's your call, of course...Just a word to the wise."

ALWAYS KEEP YOUR FULL POLICY FOR YOUR FILE—PRIVATE AND GROUP

Once you secure your private specialty own occupation coverage, the top insurance companies nowadays issue their policies electronically (PDF usually). It's important that you keep the full policy on your electronic device or cloud (and backed up as well). While this may seem to go without saying, I need to say it because I regularly talk with physicians who want me to help them evaluate their coverage, but they don't know exactly what they have and don't have anything official on file except possibly a recent invoice. Nothing substantive (amounts, definitions, terms, etc.) is in writing. They've moved multiple times in the last decade, and any paper versions just got lost.

In their defense, I've found that often the agent they worked with never actually delivered the full policy to them. Some insurance agents appear to have a practice of *not* giving their clients the full policy. They don't want their clients either (a) reading the policy for themselves and/or (b) being able to share the policy details with another broker for examination. So instead, they'll provide a summary, a Word doc snapshot, or a quote. But none of this confirms your policy was issued and what the terms of the coverage are.

It's okay—and highly advisable, actually—to insist that you have a full policy copy on hand. Then take the time to be sure your policy says what you think it says. Even though you're not the insurance expert, you need to read and ask questions for any parts you don't understand.

If this is your first contract, you'll want to confirm that when you go to increase your policy's coverage in the future, you'll get the same definitions and rate structure. Be sure this is in writing. A couple of fringe companies do not guarantee the definitions or the rate structure when you increase. This is something to avoid if possible.

OTHER QUALITIES OF A GOOD BROKER

A good disability broker will help you with essentially every-thing regarding your coverage: securing the best coverage with the maximum discounts, making sure your address is updated, helping when you want to increase your coverage, even making sure that your claims process is going as it should. Unfortu-nately, many—if not most—of the people in my business only do the minimum.

So be sure to do your own research before you start working with a broker. Ask around and talk to a colleague about who they used. For one thing, you want to make sure you're work-ing with someone who is truly independent, meaning that none of the major companies pay their overhead. It's reason-able to ask a broker straight up, "Hey, I know you say you're independent, but can you explain to me what independence means to you?"

IS YOUR BROKER INDEPENDENT, REALLY?

When it comes to finding a trustworthy broker, you want to identify someone who puts your care and interests at the top of their priority list. You want their ultimate allegiance to be with you. There are essentially four types of disability insur-ance brokers you'll come across.

First, there is the captive agent who works for a single insurance company. They give up a significant portion of whatever commissions they earn to the insurance company. In exchange, the insurance company usually pays some or all of their overhead. For this exchange, the agent is required to sell that company's insurance policies.

Occasionally, these agents are allowed to quote other companies. However, their compensation structure makes this complicated and much less desirable for the agent. They may say they are "independent," but they are highly incentivized to sell one particular company's products. In other words, all roads typically lead back to their captive company's policy. It's *buyer beware* when it comes to the independence and expertise of this type of agent.

Second, there is the general financial planner who manages assets (mutual funds, etc.), does retirement planning, helps with college education funding, budgeting, and possibly estate planning. They'll sometimes broker disability policies to either help an existing financial planning client or as a point of entry to gain a new client. As discussed earlier in the book, this is what I used to do. A "jack of all trades, master of none" type.

Some generalists are better than others, of course, but their focus day in and day out is usually not disability coverage: the options, up-to-date discounts, medical underwriting, making sure you know about additional coverage options, assisting with claims adjudication, etc. But since some physicians don't know who else to turn to for help, they'll go with a generalist. Which is understandable. I've helped a number of financial planners with questions about private specialty coverage and client situations they come across.

The third type of broker is one who's part of a consulting or brokerage firm. You'll run into these folks often if you work at a health system or larger practice, or even certain GME offices. This category can also include online quote engines. These firms have certain policies they offer (which can include the top-tier contracts but also some not in the top tier), and there's usually a rep you can talk to if you're wanting to buy. Then, after you buy and become a policyholder, often you're passed along to another department within the consulting/brokerage firm and/or given an 1-800 number to call if you ever need help. The good news is the consulting/brokerage firm is usually larger and perhaps they have a "known name." Also, their onboarding process can be relatively easy. The not-so-good news is it can be like doing business with so many other large companies: if/when you need help, you're essentially on your own.

Then, fourth, there is the independent broker who sets up their own office and pays their own overhead. Ideally, they invest in a robust support team for processing, client care, etc. They're usually independent, meaning that they find and confirm the best insurance contracts and establish relationships with these companies. Then they bring these top-tier options directly to you as the end buyer to decide for yourself which is best. If the broker is good, they'll gain access to each company's largest trainee discounts.

This is the type of broker I am. You may see this as good, or you may prefer one of the other types. But having seen all of these types behind the scenes during my thirty-plus year insurance career, I wouldn't trade where I am for anything else.

I'm saying this because it's important for you as a physician and policyholder—the one with your and your family's financial future on the line with this policy—to know which broker is best for your preferences. You will likely have your disability policy for a long time. You'll also likely move away from your training location to a different part of the country or world, meaning even if you started with a local person, you'd be working long distance with whoever your broker is. And if a claim is filed, you will want to know that you're being cared for by someone who truly has worked for you from the beginning.

I'm not going to lie, I'd love to work with every trainee in the country. But, obviously, that's not realistic. So as a second option, I just want to be sure you know the lay of the land as you find your broker.

The best brokers will stay involved. They'll be responsive and dependable. And if you pick the right one, you might actually like them.

THE BROKER'S ROLE DURING A CLAIM

The top specialty own occupation disability policies are very strong contractually. The companies that offer them are generally excellent at the time of a claim. And although these companies will be communicating with you directly (for HIPAA reasons) during a claim, your broker can be as involved in the claims process as you want them to be. You will just have to sign an authorization for the broker to discuss your claim with the insurance company.

Of course, you can choose to navigate a claim by yourself. Or you might be forced to go it alone if you don't know who your broker is or if they have left the insurance business (which happens a lot). If possible, it's advisable to consider having someone you know and trust—ideally an expert—advocating for you during this process. Here's an example of why.

A client of mine named Michael is an emergency physician who worked in a very high-stress emergency room. He was also a medical director for another facility. He did well financially but was paying a severe personal cost for it. About two years ago, Michael had a stroke that caused him to go blind in one eye. He missed work for about six months and eventually went back to work part-time in the medical director role. But he was deathly afraid to intubate anyone with only one eye working. And he was also suffering from severe anxiety/PTSD related to the work situation, the trauma surrounding his stroke, and the impact all of this was having on his family.

So even though he was back to work, his income was still a lot less than before the stroke.

Michael had contacted me about filing a claim shortly after the stroke. We got him everything he needed and then kept in touch periodically to make sure he was doing okay and the claim process was moving along smoothly. Then one day he called me and said, "Billy, I just got a letter saying they have denied my claim." I could hardly believe what I was hearing (we've not had a client's claim denied before) and asked him what happened. He explained the situation as best he could and then said, "I don't know what to do. I guess I'll just drop this insurance since it's no good anyway." He was ready to call it quits on ever getting a benefit.

I begged him to hold off on canceling for a few weeks and let me do some investigating on my end. I said if I couldn't move the needle on his behalf, then I'd help him cancel his policy. He agreed. Shortly after, I called and spoke with the insurance company claims representative (David) who told me the situation based on the information he had received from Michael's physicians. David said that even though Michael appeared to have significant pain and symptoms (blindness in one eye, PTSD symptoms, etc.), his medical records did not reflect that these were disabling. Apparently, Michael had left out many important details about his condition when talking to the doctors overseeing his care. So, the medical records David was reading were not as detailed as they should be, which caused the claim to be denied.

I called Michael back, and after talking with him at length, I became convinced this was a case of the details being "lost in translation." Michael desperately wanted to get better. I could tell when I spoke to him that he absolutely hated the thought of being disabled. To compensate for this, he was unknowingly being less-than-forthcoming to his physicians, as if it wasn't "that big of a deal." Without knowing it, he had become his own worst enemy.

With this in mind, I suggested to Michael that if he wanted his claim to be reopened (which David offered to do right away if new information was provided), he needed to go back to his doctors and clarify in detail the full situation. I told Michael, "Just be honest. It's okay to reveal what's really going on." To his credit, Michael went back and did exactly that. The records were updated and sent to David, who then approved the claim.

Michael then called me back and told me the good news: "Hey, Billy, I just received a letter saying my claim has been approved, and it includes a check that covers this month and the previous four months going back to when the elimination period ended. Thank you, man!"

Obviously, the circumstances of any claim will be investigated individually, and policy benefit eligibility will be determined based on the contract language of the policy when it was issued. Brokers are not miracle workers. But I share this as a real-life example of the impact your broker can have. A disability claim—like life in general—is not always cut and dry. It's usually emotional, and it can also be confusing and/or complicated. You don't know what you don't know. Make sure your broker is someone who knows at least some of what you don't know. Work with an expert because, again, they can be as involved as you want them to be.

HOW YOUR BROKER IS PAID

It is my professional opinion that insurance companies who offer disability policies would get rid of brokers and go direct to the public (i.e., you the buyer) if they could. So why don't they? They're doing it with car and homeowner's insurance (how many TV commercials do we see regularly), and some companies are also trying to do it with term life insurance. So why not disability insurance?

From what I've seen in my three decades in the insurance business, a big reason is because there are not enough people who follow through with buying disability insurance without a broker reminding them (proactively and hopefully politely) to do so. Disability insurance is complicated enough that even if you did decide to buy it on your own, you likely would reach the point of needing—and demanding—the help of an expert, someone who is knowledgeable about the details.

Regarding compensation, the broker gets paid a relatively small percentage of the premium you pay for the life of your policy. This fee—commonly referred to as a commission—is already built into the cost of your policy. Under the current structure, if you contacted a top disability insurance company directly to purchase a policy, they would likely send you to a broker like me. There has to be a broker on the application.

If you pay the policy premium for thirty years, the broker is paid this commission for thirty years. This happens even if you never speak to your broker again after buying the policy. The essential reason for this is to incentivize the broker to try to keep you happy. It's up to you to make them earn it.

THE ABCS OF INSURANCE

I had a call recently with a new client, a female physician who was about to finish training. She said, "I just need some very basic information. What is the insurance for? What happens? How does it pay?" When I talk to someone like this, it's striking how little exposure they've had to insurance. Even though they may lack even a basic understanding of these concepts, I appreciate how honest they are about it. It takes a lot of courage to reach out to someone and ask for help when you're not even sure why you need it.

In the case of this particular physician, she just hadn't spent any time thinking about insurance or what she'd need to do if she ever became disabled. She spent the last decade covered up in studying and engaged in her training. So, we started at ground zero and talked about the ABCs of disability insurance. We discussed why it's worth even thinking about. Then, we talked more about the important definitions in the best contracts and which companies offered them.

After about forty-five minutes, she said, "I feel like I've probably already forgotten a lot of what you told me. Do you have anything you can send me that covers all this information?"

I said, "Sure, I'll send you a summary of everything. I'm going to give you a spreadsheet with terms and discounted rates for each top company, each point defined, as well as a sample contract for you to review. I'll highlight the page numbers for the vital definition and riders. Then we can discuss it again in as much detail as you'd like."

If you're talking with a broker and they can't show you where in the contract to find a piece of information and read it with you, then you should look for a different broker. And if they can't back up what they're telling you in writing with the contract, then you *really* need to find someone else.

As I work with more and more physicians who are not born here and who speak English as a second language, many of them are new to the whole concept of insurance. They've been told they need to get it, but that's about all they know. Their questions are very basic, like "What is a premium? What does that mean? How do I pay?" They have a limited understanding of the term *own occupation*, how the COLA rider works, how the elimination period comes into play, and even the difference between post-tax and pre-tax. They're having to learn all these things from scratch.

When I'm involved in these types of conversations, we start with the basics and work from there. It takes what it takes—sometimes it's three or four conversations over the phone and via email. Other times it's less. And other times they end up saying, "Just tell me what to do to get this right."

It's humbling to me to realize they're counting on me to help them not mess it up, from a definition and a cost standpoint. This responsibility is very serious. My sole focus with them is to make sure they get this part of their financial life right. The best disability brokers care about this the most.

YOU NEED A SPECIALIST—A *GOOD* ONE

Let me use an analogy. Say you're getting a knee replacement. Sure, a general surgeon can probably figure out what needs to be done, but that's not who I—and likely you—would want to go to. The general surgeon may have even performed a knee replacement in the past and is likely smart enough to do the necessary research to make sure it goes okay. But a *specialist* will have performed the same exact surgery on thousands of knees. It's what they do all day, every day. They're masterful at it. Most likely, *they're* the person you would want to see for your knee replacement.

It's the same with specialty own occupation disability insurance. Yes, a financial advisor or general insurance agent can probably figure it out *if* they take the time to research it. But do you really want to risk your entire financial future on someone who's figuring it out along the way? Of course not! Again, if you're like most of us, you'll want to go with the specialist, the person who's an expert in the subject and holds a proven track record. Getting you the information you need to make the best decision about your disability coverage isn't going to be difficult for them. It's second nature.

But you also need the *right* specialist, someone who can help move the needle for you when things get complicated.

For example, I had a surgeon client who needed to change the bank account from which his annual insurance premium was drafted. Easy enough, right? But due to an error, the change didn't go through, and the client happened to be out of the country when his annual premium came due. He didn't know that anything was wrong, so he missed the payment, even the grace period, and his policy lapsed.

The good news: because of my relationship over the years with this client's insurance company, I was able to reach out, explain what happened, and ask them to make an exception.

They didn't *have to* oblige. They had the contractual right to require this individual to completely start over, which would have meant a redo of his medical underwriting and removal of any discount. In other words, they could have totally hosed him! Instead, they reinstated his policy.

Let me say it again to be sure it's clear: who your broker is really matters.

You want someone who has experience with the right channels connecting them to underwriters, claims people, and folks who process premiums. Think of it this way: when you choose the right broker, you're working not only with them but by extension all the good people with whom they've developed connections over the years.

CHAPTER ELEVEN

THE DAY YOU HOPE NEVER COMES

REMEMBER MICHELLE FROM CHAPTER TWO?

After being diagnosed with breast cancer, she went through the claims process and got treatment. Eventually, Michelle's claim was paid out according to her policy definitions. She finished her treatment and was able to return to her job.

Back at work, she started paying her insurance premiums again. Her policy also had the future insurability option, which allowed her to further increase her coverage because her income was eventually higher than before the claim (which is not usually the case).

Having well-structured private specialty disability insurance made it possible for her to increase coverage even after being out on claim. So if the previous illness returns or another disability occurs, she'll collect a much higher amount.

Also, since she was out on claim, she's already received far more money from the insurance company than she'll ever pay in premiums. And it's not even close.

While she obviously wishes she'd never been disabled, Michelle learned firsthand how well she did in choosing her coverage in spite of her lack of excitement about getting it at all. Because she chose from among the top specialty occupation contracts, her claim-filing process was relatively smooth and ultimately successful.

The same can be true for you too. If you choose from among the top contracts and "the day you hope never comes" does in fact come, the claims process can be successful. Whether or not it goes smoothly really depends on your knowing what to expect.

READ YOUR CONTRACT

If you do incur an injury or illness and need to file a claim, take the time to review your contract again. Talk with your broker and have them tell you specifically what pages the vital definitions are on.

Keep in mind that the claims people are going to do the exact same thing when they receive your claim: pull out their copy of the contract and read it. The contract is what will govern whether or not you get paid and how much.

Again: the claims person is *not* going to say, "Send me all the emails from your broker," or "What do you think your coverage says?" or "What were you told?" Rather, they're going to read the contract. All that matters, at the end of the day, is what is in your contract.

As discussed in Chapter Ten, you can try to navigate the claim adjudication process by yourself if you want to. But to the extent you want them involved, this is where your broker should earn their money: advocating on your behalf directly to the insurance company. With the top specialty disability companies, your broker can be as involved as you want them to be.

NOT ALL COMPANIES ARE THE SAME

One of the best ways to ensure your claims process goes smoothly is to work with pleasant people if at all possible. As simple as it sounds, it's still worth saying. Hopefully, you've chosen a pleasant broker, and if they are as good as you expect them to be, they'll be able to tell you about the culture and people at these insurance companies. They'll also be able to tell you how rigid or flexible a company is in terms of getting things done.

As I'm sure you know, different companies have different corporate cultures. I have clients who ask me, "Are certain companies easier to deal with?" This is an excellent question.

And my answer is: "Of course." It's like anything else. You can walk into certain stores and if they know you're a loyal customer or business partner, right away they are welcoming and warm; the people working there have a "Let's figure out a way to make it work" approach to how they do things. It's in their corporate culture, in their DNA, you might say. Then, you can walk into other stores and feel like, *Wow, they really don't care who I am or if I'm here at all.* Again, it's just how the culture is there.

The culture at some insurance companies is cold and rigid. This doesn't mean their contract won't pay claims. And it's not that the people who work there are bad people. For the most part, they're probably very good people. But imagine working at a gigantic insurance company that has been in existence for 150 years. I'm not kidding. Most of these insurance companies are almost 200 years old! So when I say they have a certain culture, we're talking about a culture that has been around for a long time.

They have a certain way of doing things, and most of the people who work there do not have the authority to deviate very far from their manual on how things are done. Even for good business partners (i.e., brokers who bring them a lot of business), they can have little ability to make exceptions for unusual circumstances. While they can still be very reliable, they come across as a bit colder in how they do things.

Conversely, a few other companies—often a little smaller in size—will hold your hand more. Their culture encourages their leaders to be more creative and has a focus on being more nimble in supporting the growth of their business and part-ner relationships. This approach gives them an edge when competing with their humongous competitors. If you have a solid broker who does a lot of business with them, these are the companies you'll want to have if you ever need an exception.

In Chapter Ten, I mentioned the surgeon client who changed bank accounts before going overseas for an extended vaca-tion. Here's the full story. He was essentially off the grid for a month or more. Right before leaving for his trip, he sent us the form with an incorrect account number on it, which we had no way of knowing before submitting the form to the insurance company. The draft was returned, never went through, and, you guessed it, we could not get in touch with him.

The grace period passed, and the policy lapsed due to nonpay-ment. My team had sent him about a half dozen emails and several texts to get the form corrected. No response. I thought he had ghosted me!

A week or so went by, and then out of nowhere he called me in a panic and told me he just got back into town and opened his mail to find a termination letter from the insurance company. He was actually scared to death. He made it clear that the form error was a mistake and he definitely wanted to keep the policy.

But again, it was too late. His policy was terminated. If going by the book, this meant he would be required to start over from scratch with new medical underwriting that now included an insurance physical. His premium would be higher because (a) he was older and (b) he was an attending now, so he would not qualify for the trainee discount that he had had on the now-lapsed policy. Before dropping this bomb on him in full detail, I said, "Let me discuss with my contacts at the insurance company and see what the options are." He thanked me and we hung up.

Right away, I reached out to my key contact at this company and explained the situation. They did some digging, and about twenty-four hours later, I got a call from my contact. He said we got an exception—all my client needed to do was submit the corrected bank draft form, sign a "good health statement" confirming his health had not changed significantly, and pay the past due premium.

This type of exception is not easy to get and certainly not guaranteed. This is why I don't want to mention the company by name. And truthfully, my client did not factor into whether or not they gave the exception. At the end of the day, the company doesn't know him from Adam's house cat. They gave the exception (a) because they're easier to deal with and (b) because of my relationship with them.

Insurance companies cannot make a habit of reinstating lapsed policies with no evidence that the insured is still healthy. But at times they make business decisions based on the situation. Once again, who your broker is matters. And who the company is matters.

In the end, it's about preference and priorities. For example, some of my clients couldn't care less about this type of qualitative, non-numeric stuff. But for others, an icy approach is a deal breaker regardless of how strong the contract language is.

HOW TO FILE A CLAIM

For private specialty coverage, the claims process is relatively straightforward. The insured (or somebody on their behalf) notifies the insurance company and/or the insurance broker that an illness or injury has occurred and a claim needs to be filed. The paperwork is then sent—usually in hard copy as well as electronically—directly to the insured. For HIPAA reasons, insurance companies are going to initially communicate specific details about the disability with *you,* the person insured—unless, that is, you fill out an authorization form stating that your broker can discuss it with the claims person.

As mentioned in Chapter Ten and earlier in this chapter, your broker can be as involved as you want them to be. This is where they earn their pay if you're inclined to let them. Allowing them to have access to and to communicate directly with the claims coordinator can help speed up the process. Also, a good broker understands the steps and can make sure things are moving along the way they're supposed to. This can go a long way in easing your mind during this difficult time.

Remember Michael in Chapter Ten? When a claim happens, whether it's an illness or an injury, typically it's very emotional. Your life is likely never going to be the same, even if you recover. For this reason, it makes sense to think in advance of who you want to authorize to act on your behalf and contact the claims people.

Of our clients who have become disabled, I've only had one client contact the insurance company directly when they filed a claim. She went to them first but ended up coming to me because she needed my help. She didn't know what she didn't know. So she asked me to break it down for her, and ultimately we were able to get her questions answered.

You'll still be responsible for filling out the paperwork (including an updated HIPAA form) and sending it back to the insurance company. Of course, you'll also need to provide the details of your illness or injury and the names of (and contact info for) the physicians overseeing your care.

When you send in your completed forms, this opens the claims file and activates the insurance company to start collecting medical records. The claims department then begins communicating directly with your physicians to obtain your records. This process can take several weeks. It can seem like forever, but it's just the normal time lag to get a full file and picture of the situation.

Eventually, they'll interview you. They'll ask what happened and what life is like for you now. If your contract is structured properly with the true specialty's own occupation coverage, the claims person will also ask you detailed questions about your specific job and duties. They'll ask about a typical day in your work life: did you drive to work, what time would you arrive, how long would you be there, and what are all the tasks you did during the day?

If you're a gastroenterologist specializing in endoscopies, maybe during your career you've been trained to do thirty tasks, but in your current practice, you have five duties that you perform over and over. These duties are then confirmed via the treatment/procedural codes filed for patients you treat.

If you can't perform the material parts of these five duties, then the question is, "Are you considered totally disabled?"

If you have a specialty own occupation disability insurance policy, the answer will be yes because those five duties are the essence of your specific occupation. If you can't do them, you're disabled.

But if you *don't* have specialty occupation disability insurance, all bets are off. Depending on which disability definition your policy actually does include, it can get muddy because, in theory, you could then go do one of the twenty-five other duties you've been trained in. In these cases, you can expect the claims person to actually use your extensive training against you. They're going to say, in essence, "Okay, so you can't do these five things anymore, but you're still smart and highly trained. Go do one or more of these other twenty-five duties, and in the meantime, we're not going to classify you as totally disabled."

The good news: if you answered the questions honestly in the claims interview, and your physician was able to confirm what you said, then the next step will usually be approval from the insurance company. All you'll have to do at that point is wait out your elimination period (which could be anywhere from ninety to 180 days, depending on your selection).

And that's it. Soon you'll start receiving your benefits.

WHY I'M HERE

WHEN I WAS GROWING UP, THERE WERE CERTAIN PEOPLE I looked up to: police officers, firemen, and physicians. Even now, I still admire those who choose these paths because they are committed to helping others.

Physicians are often the smartest people in their classrooms in grade school and college. They usually study really hard and complete extensive training so they can care for people in ways that nobody else can. They have the information and expertise that people need at the time they need it the most.

From what I can tell, as a nation we need way *more* physicians, not less. They're not like attorneys, where we could go a few years or decades without ever needing a new one. But without physicians, it is quite likely we'd deteriorate as a society.

When I started in the insurance and financial planning business in 1991, everybody wanted to work with doctors. If you had a client base made up of physicians, you were highly regarded in our business because you were working with people who were elevated. And that meant you were elevated too.

Honestly, I never thought this would be me. I never dreamed I would work with physicians, like I do now. When I was younger, I was a bit intimidated by doctors. I don't have doctors in my family. My dad's a doctor, but the PhD version, not the MD version.

As I progressed in my career, it wasn't until I started focusing on disability insurance that I began to work with a lot of physicians. It became clear that this was the one area where physicians, who helped so many people, needed the most help themselves.

They were like sheep without a shepherd. They were lost, unsure who to turn to or trust, seeming to have little hope of ever knowing for sure they had gotten it right. I came to realize that, as brave as they may seem, physicians have significant needs too.

Doctors have a lot of skills and also a lot of pressure on them. If most people have a bad day, it may mean they don't get the sale, the car repair costs more than they expected, or something relatively small doesn't go their way. But if a doctor has a bad day, someone they were treating may have died. They live with that pressure all the time.

Because I knew people in my industry were specifically pursuing physicians, I also knew without a doubt that these doctors were not sure who to trust. There are a lot of sharks out there—I wouldn't trust a lot of insurance agents and brokers I've met either.

Ultimately, it all worked out, and I found my sweet spot, becoming the go-to expert for physicians who wanted the best disability insurance.

After working in disability insurance for a while, I had a client who asked me to go into business with him. He's a surgeon and could be the mayor of any town he lives in. When I met him, he was in his late thirties. We talked like we'd been friends for years because he's a personable guy.

One day, he asked me, "You make a ton of money, don't you?"

I said, "What do you mean?"

"You're so good at this. You must be killing it."

He was, and still is, so direct. It was like a couple of guys having a beer or sitting over coffee. He just didn't have any shyness to him.

He said, straight out, "We need to go into business together. I can get you in front of a ton of doctors, and God knows we need a lot of help. We are disasters when it comes to financial stuff. I'm good at one thing. If I reach my hand out during surgery and that nurse or assistant doesn't put the right instrument in my hand, I have no idea where to find it. I'm useless. Doctors are good at being doctors; you're good at doing *this*."

"The Suits constantly pursue us. But you," he continued, "you're different. You're relaxed." He gestured to my outfit. I wore slacks and a jacket but no tie. I never wear a tie. "You've just got it, man. That makes people want to talk to you and want to trust you. You're good at explaining this stuff."

He was serious about going into business. He went on to say, "If we do this, Billy, you're going to have to be the guy they talk to. You can't schlep them off to somebody else. They need to deal with you because *you're* the key. You're the guy."

As we talked about going into business, I felt compelled to tell him about my financial failures in the past because I didn't want him to think that I was some kind of self-made millionaire that had no bruises. I didn't want him to believe that I was further along than I was. It's impossible to have an authentic relationship with people when they don't know who you really are. I shared some of the details with him about failing at selling retirement plans and trying and failing at real estate and coming back to the insurance industry because it was familiar and I was good at it—and I needed to pay some bills.

And he said, "That's even more reason for you to do this. You've got a humility to you. I felt it before, but your story solidified it."

At this moment, it hit me that all those years I just trudged through being an average generalist were preparation for my focus on disability insurance for physicians. What my client said to me back then meant more to me than he will ever realize. It's like he breathed life into me in a way that I'll never forget.

I believe that God designs us for a specific purpose, and this is my purpose. In the movie *Chariots of Fire*, Olympic marathoner Eric Lidell says, "God made me fast. When I run, I feel his pleasure." As weird as it may sound, I feel God's pleasure when I'm talking to someone about disability insurance. My faith is important to me, but I've never felt called to go into full-time ministry or missions or become a monk (thank goodness).

At the risk of sounding goofy, since I started focusing on disability insurance for physicians, it's as if God said, "I want you to do this, and I want you to be the best at it." From that point on, my goal hasn't been to become the biggest broker on the planet. Rather, my goal has been—and still is—to become the *best* broker on the planet.

I just wanted to share some of the heart behind why I do what I do and why I love it.

DOCTORS AND THE PANDEMIC

When the COVID pandemic happened, at first I wasn't sure what was going to happen—nobody was. Very quickly, though, I realized that doctors—many of them my clients—were going to continue heading into hospitals and clinics to care for people who needed it. The world was shutting down and watching the news. But physicians were going to work.

I also saw that residents and fellows were continuing their training and heading toward graduation and becoming attendings. What we found was that a lot of younger physicians in training, who still had significant time left before graduation, started thinking about insurance earlier than they had planned on thinking about it.

It's common for trainees with several years left in training to try to put off buying disability insurance until they're further along and can hopefully afford it more. While a risky approach, I understand their mindset.

But they saw that nothing had changed in their training schedule or work requirement, and in many cases, they had more responsibility now. They had to go to the hospitals, and they weren't sure what was going to happen to them in the near (let alone the distant) future.

So I had numerous conversations with these newer trainees about how to set up their coverage in the most affordable way for their situation. It was an interesting dynamic as no one really knew what was going on with COVID and how it would progress. But these young physicians—barely making minimum wage and carrying boatloads of medical school debt—were now realizing they needed insurance ASAP because they were the ones going into the hospitals with this strange virus going around.

I spoke with an orthopedic surgeon resident who was a new client. He didn't usually work with sick people in a hospital, but he found himself on call at the hospitals in his area during the height of quarantine. His employer said, "Hey, if this stuff gets bad, your number's going to be picked at some point. You may have to come in."

Since the pandemic, when clients are buying their insurance, they'll ask me, "If I catch COVID, would that be covered?"

I'm glad I can respond, "As long as you don't have COVID when you apply, you'll be good. Ideally, you need to get it before it ever happens. But if you've had it and fully recovered, you can get covered without it being excluded."

It's important to note that this answer could change. If scientists and doctors discover longer-term side effects from COVID, insurance companies will adjust and might exclude future COVID infections if an applicant has had it before they apply.

People also bought more life insurance. With COVID, even our healthiest and youngest clients started realizing that they're limited and that they're not going to live forever.

To keep the mood light, I'd joke with my clients and say, "I bet you didn't know when you signed up to become a doctor that you were entering active duty." While they weren't usually in the military, they were still serving.

I work with pulmonologists and critical care doctors, and they were in the ICU with people who contracted COVID, not knowing if they were going to get it too, not knowing if their patients were going to live.

It was like the part in a movie where a tragic event is happening and everybody's running in one direction to get away. When 9/11 happened, you saw all those people running away from the towers, but you also saw a select few who were running toward them. The EMTs, firefighters, police—they were running into the chaos while everybody else was running away. During COVID, doctors were the same way. They answered the call to serve.

DISABILITY INSURANCE: MAKING THE RIGHT DECISION

Hopefully, this book has made the various aspects of a disability insurance policy easier to understand. But this book is not meant to replace the importance of working with an expert broker before purchasing a policy.

If you called an insurance company directly and said, "I want to buy disability insurance but not go through the broker," they'd say, "There has to be a broker assigned to the policy. You're going to pay the same rates anyway." In fact, they would send you to me or someone like me because the broker commission is "baked" into the contract. The broker is paid a small piece of the premium for the life of the policy. This is meant to incentivize your broker to try to keep you happy. The broker should be set up to help you at every step throughout your career, from time of purchase to changing addresses to increasing coverage to filing a claim. You don't pay any extra fee to receive services from a broker.

Ultimately, there are only a handful of top-tier specialty own occupation disability contracts. If they are structured correctly and contain the riders and definitions we've covered in this book, any of those top contracts would serve you well.

So many of my clients—maybe even the majority nowadays— end up asking me which one I think they should pick. When I'm asked this, I advise people as if they were my brother or my sister. I picture my sister coming to me and saying, "Hey, Billy, help me figure this out. Apparently, I need to get disability insurance. Just tell me which one to get."

This is a responsibility I take very seriously. I give them the advice they ask for. I say something to the effect of, "If I was in your situation, or you were my sister in this situation, knowing what I know, this is what I would advise. Whether you know the details of it or not is ultimately okay because I know the details. If you pick one of the contracts that we've discussed in detail, you're going to be well served. Please hear me, you need to read the contract, but even if you don't, you're going to be in good shape."

Bottom line: if you get the broker right, you can have the best coverage even if the content of this book is still confusing. Now that's good news!

If you have any questions about disability insurance, go to OwnOCCDisability.com.